# Him Big God Day

## Other books by Stanley M. Maxwell

*The Man Who Couldn't Be Killed*

*The Man Who Lived Twice*

*Prisoner for Christ*

# Him Big God Day

## And Other Remarkable Sabbath Stories

# Stanley M. Maxwell

Pacific Press® Publishing Association
Nampa, Idaho
Oshawa, Ontario, Canada
www.pacificpress.com

Cover design by Steve Lanto
Cover illustration by Dreamstime.com
Inside illustrations by James Converse
Inside design by Aaron Troia

The author assumes full responsibility for the accuracy of all facts and quotations as cited in this book.

Additional copies of this book are available by calling toll-free 1-800-765-6955 or by visiting http://www.adventistbookcenter.com.

Scriptures quoted from KJV are from the King James Version.

Scriptures quoted from NKJV are from The New King James Version, copyright © 1979, 1980, 1982, Thomas Nelson, Inc., Publishers.

Library of Congress Cataloging-in-Publication Data:

Maxwell, Stanley M., 1958-
Him Big God Day and other remarkable Sabbath stories / Stanley M.
Maxwell.
    p. cm.
ISBN 13: 978-0-8163-2617-4 (pbk.)
ISBN 10: 0-8163-2617-7 (pbk.)
1. Sabbath—Anecdotes.  2. Seventh-day Adventists—Biography.  I. Title.
BX6154.M37 2011
263'.2—dc23
                                                        2011039918

11 12 13 14 15 • 5 4 3 2 1

# Contents

# Dedication

To my wife, Phemie,
to my mother,
and to Roxy and Nigel

# Behind the Stories

The road that leads *Him Big God Day, and Other Remarkable Sabbath Stories* to your door has indeed been long and winding. The road begins with a five-year-old boy with a desire to write stories for children. He wrote quite a few, but it would be six years before one of them saw the printed page in *Junior Guide.*\*

Collecting stories initially began at the dining table. Mr. Stan's father, Dr. C. Mervyn Maxwell, author and chairman of the Church History Department at Andrews University, loved to invite guests over for Sabbath lunch. Much of the time he'd tell stories at the table about Adventist, early church, or Reformation history. When he'd finished telling church history stories, he'd ask his guests if they'd had experiences during which they'd had difficulty keeping the Sabbath and God had come to their rescue. The guests shared their stories, and Mr. Stan listened.

Mr. Stan's big break came when David Gemmell asked Mr. Stan to join with him on his new radio program *Family Picnic* on WAUS. He wanted a five-minute children's story for the family to listen to as they

---

\* Stanley Maxwell, "The Man Who Rode to California on a Potato," *Junior Guide,* October 14, 1970, 15, 18.

wiggled their toes in the grass and ate their picnic lunch. With the radio program, Mr. Stan the storyteller was born.

Thinking an adventurous life would make his stories more interesting, Mr. Stan took jobs in Thailand, China, Hong Kong, Kyrgyzstan, Macau, Jordan, and Austria, where he collected stories. He collected more stories in his travels to Africa, Asia, Europe, the Middle East, the Americas, the Caribbean, and the Galápagos Islands.

Book writing began as Mr. Stan tried to share his stories with a world-wide audience and resulted in *The Man Who Couldn't Be Killed, The Man Who Lived Twice,* and *Prisoner for Christ.* After reading *Prisoner for Christ,* a Chinese story Mr. Stan collected while working in Hong Kong, Miss Brenda of the Micheff sisters arranged for Mr. Stan to tell holiday stories in the 3ABN studios. He also taught the storytelling honor for master guides in the Uncle Arthur's grandson's storytelling booth during the Oshkosh Pathfinder camporee. He is a regular storyteller at Michigan camp meeting.

The stories in *Him Big God Day, and Other Remarkable Sabbath Stories* come in four categories: (1) stories about people who had difficulties keeping the Sabbath and God honored their faith—even in recent times; (2) stories in which something remarkable occurred on the Sabbath; (3) stories in which people's lives were altered after they witnessed the Sabbath being honored; and (4) stories designed to help readers see how some people keep the Sabbath. Often the names and occasionally the places have been changed to protect the innocent. These stories are oral stories based on memory. Mr. Stan tells them the way they were related to him.

These powerful stories about the Sabbath and about God will bless you spiritually.


Stanley M. Maxwell
May 25, 2011


PS: If you have any stories you'd like to share with Mr. Stan, please send them to him through Pacific Press®. He is always collecting good stories.

# Him Big God Day

An Australian supervisor watched a little woodcutter come from the jungles of Papua New Guinea and enter his colonial lumberyard. He asked the woodcutter his name and what he wanted.

"You callin' me Umie. Me wantin' him big boss man givin' me good workin' here," the woodcutter said.

The supervisor led the dark-skinned woodcutter into his office and explained, "We'll pay you. You cut trees, mate, and stack 'em over there." He pointed to the lumberyard outside the office window. "First, put your thumbprint here on this page." The supervisor opened an ink pad and placed it on the desk.

Umie could neither read nor write, but trusting the white man, he pressed his thumb onto the ink pad, then rolled his thumb across the bottom of the paper. He didn't know the contract required him to work six days a week from Monday to Saturday for three consecutive months, and that if he missed a single day of work, he'd be thrown into jail. But even if he could've read the contract, the word *jail* would've meant nothing to such a child of the forest.

When Umie smudged the page, the supervisor smiled. "There, now you work for us, mate." He led Umie to his barracks. "Rest t'day, work tomorrow. G'day, mate!"

The next morning, Umie trekked into the forest with the other work-ers. He enjoyed cutting trees and stacking logs.

All went well until he awoke one morning and knew it was the sev-enth day of the week. On that day he would think about God and not work. While the workers dressed, Umie lay in bed thinking about God.

The supervisor burst into the room and rushed to Umie's bedside. "Aye, mate, rise 'n' shine! There's work to be done."

Umie looked up at the supervisor. "Me no workin' this day."

"What's wrong?" The Australian looked concerned. "Are you ill?"

"This day Him Big God Day," Umie explained. "Me restin' from me workin', and me thinkin' 'bout me Big God."

The supervisor laughed, thinking the woodcutter, who had never seen a calendar, had made a mistake. "You're all mixed up. Tomorrow's the Lord's Day. T'day you work—Sunday you rest. Now, off to work, mate!"

"This day me no workin'," Umie replied. "Preacher man, 'e teachin' me from him Big Black Book. 'E tellin' me day seven is rest day of Him Big God. This day me no workin'."

The supervisor grabbed Umie angrily, dragged him out of bed, set him on his feet, and slapped his left shoulder. "You get ready for work!" he shouted.

Scared that the supervisor would strike him again, Umie covered his face with his elbow. Misunderstanding the motion and thinking Umie meant to fight back, the supervisor whipped out his knife and slashed Umie's arm. The cut bled so badly that the woodcutter couldn't have worked that day if he'd wanted to. So the supervisor let him lie in bed and think about God.

The injury healed quickly. By Monday, Umie was again cutting tim-ber and stacking lumber. On Friday, the supervisor said, "I'll make ya a deal, mate. The colonial inspector of agriculture, Dr. Spencer, arrives on the morrow. I don't want any trouble. If you'll work tomorrow, I prom-ise you'll never have to work on Saturdays again."

Umie said nothing, but when he awoke the next morning, he lay in bed, thinking about God. The supervisor stomped into the room as he had the previous week and marched over to Umie. "Get up, mate. The inspector's here, and we made a deal!"

"Sorry, me no workin' this day." Umie remained in bed.

"You tell 'im, man!" the other workers chorused in, eager to see another fight between the supervisor and the woodcutter. The supervisor lifted Umie out of bed just as Dr. Spencer, the inspector, walked in, and asked, "What's the problem?"

"This woodcutter," the supervisor pointed at Umie, "refuses to work. His rebellion is causing insurrection among the workers."

"I'll handle this," Dr. Spencer said. "Why won't you work?"

"Me no workin'. This day Him Big God Day," the woodcutter explained. "Me restin' and me thinkin' about Him Big God."

"You must work t'day. Tomorrow's yer day off." When Umie still refused, Dr. Spencer pounded his fist into the woodcutter's left shoulder. To protect himself, Umie immediately flung his right elbow over his face, surprising the inspector. Fearing an attack, Dr. Spencer beat the little woodcutter until he slumped to the floor and appeared dead. Then he kicked Umie in the ribs repeatedly until his temper subsided.

Umie couldn't work that day either. Again he lay in bed, thinking about God.

By Monday, Umie's bruises had healed enough for him to work. But Dr. Spencer summoned a local police officer, who handcuffed Umie, loaded him with all of the inspector's supplies, and ordered him to walk several miles to the nearest jail. The police officer escorted Umie, toting a rifle to prevent him from escaping. Dr. Spencer, who had completed his inspection, walked with them.

Going to jail was not easy. It meant trekking through the jungle from the lumberyard into town. All went well, however, until the three men came to a fallen log that spanned a rushing river. Umie and the police officer, both being children of the forest and accustomed to traveling in the jungle, glided over it easily, despite the loads on their backs.

Then it was Dr. Spencer's turn. He hazarded a couple of cautious steps onto the mossy log, slipped slightly, but regained his balance.

Fearful that Dr. Spencer's next step might prove disastrous, the police officer set his rifle down and ran across the log to aid the white man.

"What are you doing?" Dr. Spencer yelled. "Guard the prisoner! He may escape or grab your gun and shoot us!" Obediently, the police officer dashed back and resumed guard duty.

Dr. Spencer reached the middle of the log safely, but when he glanced below and saw crocodile snouts in the river, he panicked and leaped the rest of the way. He landed on the bank, but one foot fell into an animal hole, twisting it, and fracturing his leg. The pain grew intense.

"You wantin' me runnin' to him big city and fetchin' two fellas come helpin' you?" the police officer volunteered after examining the inspector's leg.

"What? Leave me with this criminal? He might escape or kill me." Dr. Spencer clenched his teeth and favored his broken leg.

"You wantin' him Umie fetchin' two fellas come helpin' you?" the police officer asked.

"What? Send a criminal into the woods to find help? He'll escape!"

Just then, the little woodcutter bent down and, despite his handcuffs, picked some leaves, knelt beside Dr. Spencer, and rubbed the leaves against his broken leg.

" 'E usin' 'em leaves for soothin' your heapin' big pain," the local police officer explained. Dr. Spencer noticed that indeed the pain subsided somewhat. "Remove his handcuffs!" he ordered. The police officer obeyed.

With free hands, Umie harvested more leaves and massaged the white man's legs until he felt relief. Then, even though he was heavily loaded down, Umie lifted the inspector onto his shoulder and carried him for two hours all the way to the city, where medical assistance was arranged.

* * * * *

Years later, swaying in a hammock, Dr. Spencer related this story to a Dutch colleague. "At the time, I wasn't a Christian," Dr. Spencer concluded, "though I'd been raised one. I thought that woodcutter who wouldn't work on God's Day and who massaged my leg two days after I had beaten him senseless, was a true Christian, if I'd ever seen one. God threw that little woodcutter in my path for a reason. His example shouted louder than a slew of sermons. Now I cherish his brand of Christianity for myself!"

# Fed by a Cat

**D**uring wartime, a young Seventh-day Adventist named Pieter was drafted into military service. After reporting for duty at boot camp, he soon found himself rising every morning before the first cock crowed, running laps, polishing shoes, shining buckles, doing push-ups and sit-ups. For the rest of the day, he learned to march and obey orders without thinking. If his officer shouted, "Jump, ladies!" rather than being insulted, he'd instantly reply, "How high, sir?" Then he would leap into the air to an imaginary dot. If the men wrestled, he wrestled; and if they cooked, he cooked. In no time, his unit could tolerate the daily rations and, if required, scrub floors with tooth-brushes.

Everything went on reasonably well for the first six days. But on Friday, the soldier began to think about the next day.

So he went to visit his commanding officer and was nonchalantly admitted inside his office. Saluting and speaking respectfully, he said, "Permission to speak, sir?"

Looking up from his desk, his commanding officer wearily removed his reading glasses, set them on the table atop the papers he was reading, and sighed, "Permission granted, soldier. What do you want?"

Putting on his best smile, Pieter came to the point. "Sir, I request to have tomorrow off, sir!"

The officer's face reddened. "You are there and I am here and everything is in its place. And that's how we know what is there and what is here. Everything has its place. And everyone knows his place. Do you know your place, soldier?"

"Yes, sir!" Pieter shouted.

"You do, do you, soldier?" The commanding officer cocked his head and scratched his ear with his little finger. Then he shouted, "Who do you think you are asking to have a holiday tomorrow?"

"Begging your pardon, sir!" the soldier said as he made a quick salute and clicked his heels. "Tomorrow's the day I worship God. I need the day off to study my Bible and to pray to God."

A blood vessel bulged in the officer's neck as he glared into the soldier's eyes and demanded, "What do you mean when you say, 'Study the Bible tomorrow'? Do you know what I think, Private?"

"No, sir! I don't, sir!"

"Well, I'll tell you what I think, Private Pieter."

"What's that, sir?"

"You're all mixed up, Private. Tomorrow's Saturday, not Sunday!" His eyes narrowed, "Do you think I'm that easy to fool?"

"Oh, no, sir!" The soldier exclaimed, still standing at attention. He saluted and clicked his heels again, then added softly, "Begging your pardon, sir, but I believe that God wants us to worship Him on Saturday. We call it the Sabbath because that's what God said in the Bible when He wrote the fourth commandment with His very own finger."

"What are you? A Jew?" the officer bellowed as he reached for a cup of coffee.

Not wanting to be called a Jew, the soldier stiffened involuntarily as a shiver ran up his spine. It was dangerous to be called Jewish because his officer hated Jews, often throwing them into prison because they demanded special considerations, such as kosher food. "No," the soldier asserted loudly, "I'm not a Jew—I'm a Seventh-day Adventist Christian."

The officer nearly choked on his coffee. "You're a what?"

"A Seventh-day Adventist Christian, sir," the soldier replied.

"What the dickens is a Seventh-day Adventist?"

"Seventh-day Adventists attend church on Saturday instead of on Sunday because they follow the Bible," the soldier explained.

"I've never heard such nonsense before," the officer exploded. "Did you just make up this frivolous poppycock?"

"No, sir." The soldier saluted again. "It's the truth, sir."

"I don't know if I should laugh or cry."

"No, sir! I mean yes, sir!" The soldier's head spun as he tried not to anger his commanding officer.

"Request denied!" Snatching his glasses off his desk, the officer jammed them onto his face, stood to his full height, and peered contemptuously down at Pieter. "Authority must be maintained, what? Right? Of course, right! You're in the army now, soldier. Do as I say. Now we both know each other's place. You're to report for duty, boy! And if you don't report for duty tomorrow, I'll send you to prison and put you in solitary confinement with no food—just like we do to those wretched Jews who have the gall to ask for special eating privileges. You'll remain in prison 'til you decide to obey orders. Is that understood, soldier?"

"I understand, sir!" Pieter saluted and clicked his heels again.

"Authority must be maintained."

"Yes, sir!"

"Everything has its place. And everyone knows his place. I expect you to be in your place!"

"Yes, sir!"

"Dismissed!"

Obediently Pieter turned on his heel and marched from the room.

The next day Pieter didn't turn up for duty. His commanding officer found him in his barracks reading his Bible. "You weren't in your place this morning, and it seems you've forgotten your place. And you don't respect my authority!"

Looking up from his Bible, Pieter replied, "I respect your authority, sir."

"What did I tell you about reporting for duty today? Did you think I wasn't serious?"

"Oh, no, sir!"

"Then why did you disobey a direct order?" the commanding officer demanded.

"Because I believe God wants us to worship Him on His holy day. As the apostle Peter said to the priests, 'I must obey God rather than man.' "

"Arrest him!" the commanding officer shouted. Immediately Pieter was handcuffed, marched to the other end of the compound, and unceremoniously thrown into a prison cell. When his eyes adjusted to the darkness, Pieter discovered that his cell was rather small with only one barred window placed inconveniently near the roof. It had been deliberately placed there so that no one could climb up to it. The tiny amount of light that fell upon the stone floor was striped from the shadow of the bars. The window was so tiny that no one could squeeze through it. Only a small animal could pass between the bars.

Pieter remained in the cell for a week without food. Once a day, the jailer slid a small amount of water through a trapdoor. Naturally, the soldier's stomach growled and complained, but there was nothing he could do.

After a week, the commanding officer entered the cell. "Well, I see you've lost some weight. Are you hungry?"

The soldier admitted that he was and asked for food.

Coolly, his commanding officer replied, "Are you going to obey orders?"

"Sir, if you mean, Am I going to break the Sabbath? the answer is, 'No, sir!' That is an order I cannot obey."

The commander's face flushed. "Then you will remain here with no food." Agitated, he paced the cell, shouting, "Authority must be maintained. A place for everything—and everything in its place. Right? Right!" Bending down, he lifted Pieter's chin and eyeballed him. "When you get hungry enough, you'll learn that I mean business. Then you'll obey orders." Rising to his full height, the officer stomped from the cell, slamming the door behind him. Keys rattled as his commander locked Pieter in.

Feeling alone in his cell, time dragged. About four thirty or five o'clock, he felt himself growing faint from hunger. Kneeling down on the floor, he folded his hands, closed his eyes, and prayed, "Oh, Lord, You promised that my bread and water would be sure. Last week, every day, You gave me water. Thank You. All that was missing was the bread. Today I claim the rest of Your promise. Please, make sure my bread and water are sure." As he was praying, something brushed against his leg. Finishing his prayer, the soldier opened his eyes and saw on the floor before him a slice of bread.

Picking it up, he ate it hungrily, then prayed again, thanking God for answering his prayer so quickly and miraculously.

The next day he grew hungry again at about the same time. Again he knelt down, closed his eyes, folded his hands, and prayed for food. Again he felt something brush against him. When he opened his eyes, he again saw a slice of bread on the floor, which he hungrily devoured.

This happened again and again, day after day, for two weeks.

Then the cell door opened and his commanding officer entered. "I see you're not gaunt from losing weight," the officer said. "How can this be?"

"I've been eating every day, sir," Pieter replied respectfully.

"Who's been feeding you?" the officer demanded.

"I thought you were, sir!"

"I am not!" The commander shouted and the vein in his neck began to bulge again. "I am most certainly *not*!"

"If you're not, sir, then I'm sure God must be, sir. Every day, sir, at about the same time, sir, I find a slice of bread on the floor."

"A slice of *bread* on the floor?" The commander sounded incredulous.

"That's right, sir."

"Who's feeding you this bread?"

"I don't know, sir."

"What do you mean you 'don't know'?"

"I thought you were feeding me, but I was wrong, sir. Now I don't know who it is, sir, but I'm being fed."

"Tell me what you know."

"You promise you won't be angry, sir."

"I won't be angry." The commander flashed his best smile, although one side of his mouth curled higher than the other. In a strained, patient tone, he added, "I need to know *who* is feeding you."

"Well, sir. Every day I pray for food, and while I'm praying, something brushes against my leg; and when I've finished my prayer, I find a slice of bread on the floor."

"But you don't know who is giving you this bread?"

"Honestly, sir, I don't."

"And why not?" The officer sounded slightly irritated, but gritted his teeth to keep from losing his temper.

"Because, sir, when I pray I close my eyes. And I don't open them again until I've finished the prayer."

The officer nodded his head as if he understood and finished the thought. "So you can't see what happens while you pray."

"That's right, sir." Pieter said. "Because my eyes are closed."

"Well, you find out who it is!" his commander said. "That's an order!"

"I'll do my best, sir."

"Do you think you could pray with your eyes open?"

"I think I could make an exception in this case, sir."

"You do that."

"Yes, sir!"

"That's an order. Pray with your eyes open. I'll be back tomorrow. I want to know who's feeding you."

"I'll do my best, sir, but I can't promise anything. What if it's my guardian angel? I might not see anything. I hope you understand, sir."

"I want to know who's feeding you. Do you know what I mean?"

"I do, sir." He didn't speak with as much confidence as he felt he should. He feared it was his guardian angel, and he really wouldn't see him.

The next day at about half past four or five o'clock, his stomach began to rumble again. Pieter knelt on the stone floor as was his habit. But this time he did something different. He didn't close his eyes as he prayed.

While he was praying, he saw, from the corner of his eye, a cat come to the window, squeeze between the bars, and jump to the floor. It stealthily approached him and brushed against his leg. At that point Pieter noticed that the cat was carrying something in its mouth. He couldn't believe what he saw. Blinking, he shook his head and looked again to make sure he wasn't seeing things. Sure enough, his eyes were playing no tricks. It was a slice of bread!

Awestruck, Pieter watched as the cat dropped the slice onto the floor, turned, leaped to the window, squeezed between the bars, and vanished.

Amazed, Pieter prayed again. "Thank You, Lord, for performing such a marvelous miracle just for me!" Then he picked up the slice and ate it heartily.

The next day guards came to the cell and took Pieter to the commander's office. Once inside, Pieter stood at attention, clicked his heels, and saluted the officer.

"At ease, soldier!" The commander ordered after returning the salute. Pieter obeyed. Coming straight to the point, the officer asked, "Do you know who's been feeding you?"

"I do, sir."

"Tell me who'd dare do such a thing!"

Pieter shifted his feet and stared somewhere behind the commander's head. "You're not going to believe me, sir."

"Who is it?"

"I think you'll find this hard to believe, sir."

"Just tell me the answer."

"All right, sir." Pieter inhaled deeply. "It's a cat."

"A *cat*!" the officer exclaimed incredulously.

"I thought you wouldn't believe me, sir!"

"Explain, soldier. This better be good."

"Yes, sir." Pieter licked his lips as his mouth went dry. "When I knelt down to pray yesterday, I kept my eyes open, which isn't usually my custom." His heart pounded louder than usual. "While I was praying, a cat came to the window—you're not going to believe this!"

"I'm listening, soldier."

"Promise you won't laugh, sir?"

"I promise! Tell me what happened."

"All right, sir. While I was praying, a cat came to the window carrying a slice of bread in its mouth. After jumping down from the window, it laid the slice of bread at my feet, then leaped back up to the window again, squeezed through, and vanished, sir." So certain was Pieter that the officer would accuse him of lying that his hands grew clammy. To his amazement, the commander's eyes lit up and a half smile spread across his face. *Is he going to laugh?* "Do you believe me?" Pieter asked doubtfully.

"Young man, you've just helped me solve a mystery," the officer replied.

"What mystery is that, sir?"

"What time did you say you pray for food? Is it around four thirty or five o'clock?"

"Yes, it was, sir! How'd you know?"

"My daughter's cat has been behaving very strangely this month every day at about four thirty or five o'clock."

"And what does it do, sir?"

"It begins howling in the worst way and won't stop until we give it a slice of bread. But the cat never eats it in front of us. It takes the bread and vanishes. We assumed the cat was extra hungry or had a secret litter somewhere. Now I understand—my daughter's cat has been feeding *you* with *my* bread!"

Pieter was amazed and praised God.

"If my daughter's cat is going to feed you every day with my bread," the commander continued, "I guess I'll never be able to starve you into obeying orders."

"Yes, sir!" Pieter agreed.

"That means there's no use putting you in solitary confinement, or trying to starve you into submission."

"Yes, sir!"

"It's not going to work."

"No, sir! I mean, yes, sir!"

"Your God is trying to tell me something. And that is that you need your Sabbaths off to worship Him. Well, so you shall!"

"Yes, sir! Thank you, sir!" Pieter saluted again.

"You're released. Dismissed!"

Pieter saluted, clicked his heels, and returned to his barracks.

The commander kept his word. Pieter was allowed to worship God every Sabbath as long as he was under that officer's command. And it all happened because of a powerful God who asked a cat to take a slice of bread through a prison window to feed a faithful soldier who dared to obey God rather than a stubborn officer, regardless of the consequences.

Pieter still says, "God's promises are true. If you believe and act on faith, your bread and water will be sure—even a cat can help provide for you!"

# Saved by a Picture on the Wall

In Rwanda, an African country made famous by Dian Fossey and her study of mountain gorillas, live two groups of people, the Tutsis and the Hutus. It's rather difficult to distinguish between the two groups. Some say that the average Tutsi is taller than the average Hutu, but that's not always true. At one time, when Belgium governed the land, the Belgians gave the better jobs to the Tutsis, most likely because they were better educated than the Hutus. Needless to say, the Hutus weren't too happy about this. In the 1990s, many Hutus and a significant number of Tutsis felt that they had reason to resent each other.

By 1994, the hatred between the Tutsis and the Hutus got out of control. The Hutus began attacking the Tutsis with machetes, hacking them to death. Soon, just about everyone got involved in the slaughter, including Christians. And, I'm sorry to say, even some Seventh-day Adventists took part in the mayhem, killing fellow Adventists for no reason other than that they were Tutsis.

Because the Hutus were going from house to house, looking for Tutsis to attack, a certain church member (let's call him Solomon) was, quite understandably, frightened for his life, afraid to go out, and scared to stay home. Solomon and his pregnant wife decided to hide in their attic, which was just a narrow space between the ceiling and the roof, with barely enough room for them to lie and wait. They lay there for four days and nobody came. Then they realized that it was the Sabbath, and they longed to celebrate with their traditional Sabbath bath.

Planning to return to their hiding place as soon as they had bathed, Solomon's wife went first, crawling toward the entrance of their attic. But the boards were weak, and she was heavier than usual due to her pregnancy. In an instant, she fell from the ceiling to the floor below.

Hearing the noise, Solomon crawled over to check on her and fell through himself, landing on the soft cushion of his pregnant wife.

Just then they heard a noise outside. It was the sound of stones pelting the house. To their dismay, the couple realized that they had left their hiding place just in time for a Hutu raid. As they looked into each other's frightened eyes, both had the same thought, *If only we'd stayed in the attic and forgotten about our Sabbath bath! Perhaps we should've taken our baths on Friday in preparation for the Sabbath, but it's too late now.*

They couldn't return to the attic because of the gaping hole; it would be the first place the mob looked. They had to think of something—and fast. Quickly breathing panicked prayers for God's help, they dashed into their bedroom. Solomon helped his pregnant wife squeeze beneath their bed before joining her himself.

There they lay, listening to the Hutus ransacking their home, taking everything they could grab and smashing anything they couldn't. Resisting the urge to save their beloved house and their precious belongings, the husband and wife remained motionless beneath the bed, fearful for their lives, hoping they wouldn't be discovered as the looters came closer. Eventually, the angry Hutus entered the bedroom.

Unfortunately, in his rush to hide under the bed, Solomon had lost a shoe, and it lay on the floor beside the bed. A member of the mob picked up the shoe, held it up, and shouted, "Look what I found! A shoe!" There was an awkward silence until someone at the other side of the room exclaimed, "Fool! Whatcha gonna do with just *one* shoe? You have *two* feet, don't you? Forget it!"

"I gots me two feet last I checked. You got that right," the first man concurred. "I bet the owner of this shoe has another foot too. So if I found one shoe, there must be another here somewhere. I'm gonna find it!"

"Good luck with that!" the other man laughed. "He probably escaped with it on his other foot."

Under the bed, Solomon's heart raced. He hoped he wouldn't be discovered, but feared the worst.

The looter with the shoe looked beneath the bed and declared, "I found the other shoe!" He pulled on it, but it didn't come easily. "It's attached—to a foot!"

That announcement caught everyone's attention, and they rushed to the bed. They screamed at the couple, "Come out!" But try as they might, the couple couldn't. Not only were Solomon and his wife paralyzed from panic, but the space under the bed was actually so tight that they were hopelessly stuck. Much to the couple's chagrin, the mob proved all too eager to assist them, tearing the mattress off, yanking out the bedsprings, and propping up the bed frame. Exposed like deer under headlights, Solomon and his wife lay petrified on the floor. "Stand up!" the looters yelled. Instantly, hands grabbed the hapless pair, forcing them to their feet.

"Give us your money!" the mob demanded.

"We don't have any money," Solomon replied. "We're church employees."

Not liking what they'd heard, the mob raised their machetes. Solomon and his wife closed their eyes, mentally preparing to die.

At that moment, six militiamen burst into the house and ordered the mob to leave. Seeing the militiamen's machine guns, the mob realized their machetes were useless. Instantly, they obeyed, running out the door with whatever loot they could carry.

Grateful though they were to be rid of the mob, Solomon and his wife did not feel safe. *Many of the militia also hate us Tutsis. Have these soldiers come to keep the peace or to cause more trouble?*

One of the soldiers, who appeared to be their leader, looked around the ransacked house and saw a picture still hanging in its place on the wall. Perhaps the only item remaining in the house after the mob fled, it was a framed picture of Jesus. Written above the face of Christ were the words *Seventh-day Adventist.* Turning to Solomon, the soldier asked, "Are you Christian?"

Somehow Solomon felt compelled to answer. Looking the soldier in the eye, he replied, "Yes."

"Then don't worry," the soldier said. "We won't kill you. We don't want the blood of a Christian on our hands, do we?" He turned to the other five, who immediately agreed.

Sweat dripped down the Tutsi couple's backs as relief flooded their souls.

"Is there anything we can do for you?" the leader of the soldiers asked. "It isn't safe here."

The couple nodded.

"Where would you like us to take you?"

"There's an Adventist church about five hundred yards from our home," Solomon said. "Can you take us there? It's Sabbath, so they might be holding a service."

"With this violence going on?" the soldier asked doubtfully. "Do you think anyone would be in church?"

"Perhaps not," Solomon pursed his lips, "It's difficult to say due to the present circumstances. But the pastor will be there."

"Are you sure you'll be safe?"

"The pastor is a Hutu," Solomon admitted, "but he's a good man. I know he wants to help the Tutsis. I trust him."

The militiamen agreed. The six of them surrounded the Tutsi couple like bodyguards and escorted them the short distance to the church. When they arrived, the soldiers pounded on the door. The Hutu pastor cautiously opened it a crack, recognized the Tutsi couple in the midst of the guards, and swung the door wider. "Welcome and happy Sabbath, Solomon! What can I do for you?" he asked. "Is your wife all right?"

Solomon told about the mob that had pillaged his house and threatened their lives. "I don't think it's safe at my home anymore," he asserted. "Could we stay in the church?"

"Of course, come inside." The pastor beamed as they entered. Solomon turned and thanked the soldiers, who then marched off. "We're hiding Tutsis behind the baptistry," the Hutu pastor said in a whisper as he led the couple down the aisle. "It's a tad crowded as you might imagine, but you can stay as long as it's safe."

Solomon and his wife hid there with other Tutsis for some time. The Hutu pastor never betrayed them.

One day the pastor came to their hiding spot and grimly announced, "I'm afraid it's no longer safe—even in the sanctuary of a church. You'll have to leave. But don't worry," he smiled graciously, "I've made arrangements for you."

The Hutu pastor secretly transferred the Tutsis to a hotel. Solomon and his wife were put up in room 109, where they remained for days while violence raged outside. Then, to their dismay, they heard the dreadful sound of a Hutu mob entering the hotel. The Hutus systematically broke into every room, searching for Tutsis. As they approached, the couple remained locked in their room, knowing that if they opened their door and ran for their lives, they'd attract undue attention to themselves. It would be much worse for them outside.

The mayhem reached room 105, terrorizing the Tutsis inside. Solomon and his wife resisted the urge to answer their neighbors' pleas and screams. Instead, they huddled in the corner, knowing that soon, after four more doors had been broken down, it would be their turn to die.

Suddenly, the militia arrived and ordered the mob to leave. It obeyed. Solomon and his wife had been spared yet again.

Eventually, following outside intervention from the French, the hostilities ended, and Solomon and his wife returned home and attended church again. In one church service he learned that Hutus, some of them Adventists, had killed fifty-six Tutsi Adventist pastors. Each of those pastors had been shepherds for two thousand Rwandans. Instantly, Solomon felt that he must become a minister. If only he could go to the United States to study in the theological seminary and then return to Rwanda. Then he could help replace some of the pastors killed in the carnage.

As time passed, it appeared that God was good to Solomon and his family. Despite her fall from the attic, his wife carried their child to full term and gave birth to a lovely baby boy. Later Solomon and his family were accepted to study at Andrews University and granted political asylum in the United States, thus enabling him to obtain work visas so he could afford to send his son to Ruth Murdoch Elementary School.

Looking back, Solomon is certain that God saved his family at least three times in Rwanda. Every morning Solomon reminds himself that he, his wife, and his son are living miracles—and it all began with a picture of Jesus hanging on their bedroom wall.

# Shahine's Sabbath Test

Shahine was born in Istanbul about the time Turkey became a nation. Her mother was one of the first Seventh-day Adventists in what was once the Ottoman Empire. Her father was not an Adventist; he was an Armenian Christian. Armenians are a Christian minority in an otherwise Muslim region of the world. Her father was very supportive of his wife's beliefs and allowed Shahine to be raised as an Adventist Christian.

When Shahine went to school, she was supposed to attend classes six days a week, from Monday through Saturday. But on Saturday, Shahine wanted to worship God as He'd taught His children to do in the Bible, so she didn't attend school on Sabbath. Instead, she sat in church, celebrating the wonderful things God did for His people.

Every Monday, when she returned to school, there was a note waiting for her on her desk stating that the principal wished to talk with her.

Having a pretty good idea what he wanted to see her about, she didn't particularly want to talk with him. But from respect for his position, she headed for his office anyway. After she knocked on his door, the principal opened it and welcomed her inside. He sat at his desk while Shahine stood politely, waiting for him to speak, dreading what she'd hear.

"Why didn't you come to school on Saturday?" the principal asked.

She explained to him her beliefs as a Seventh-day Adventist, saying that her religion followed the teachings of both the Old and New Testaments. "This means that I rest on Sabbath and join my fellow believers to worship as God described in the fourth commandment and through the example of Jesus. I'm a Seventh-day Adventist, so I worship on Saturday, not Sunday as most other Christians do. Sabbath is a holy day. This means that on Saturday, I attend church and I don't do any work or studying." Shahine smiled.

"I don't believe you!" the principal shouted. "I think your absence is *not* due to religion, but laziness! Remember, it's your responsibility to attend classes. Don't be lazy. You're dismissed."

Shahine bowed her head respectfully and returned to class.

The next week, on Monday, there was another note on her desk. She was called into the principal's office again. This happened week after week, until it became something of a ritual. Shahine explained that she had been at church, and the principal called her lazy, stupid, and silly for not attending school.

One Monday the principal asked her, "Can I write you a note for your pastor to sign, absolving you from church attendance so that you can attend classes?"

Shahine replied, "You don't understand. It's not the pastor forcing me to attend church. It's the Bible's teaching. God wants us to keep the day holy and to spend the day with Him. The pastor cannot exempt me from church."

On another Monday when Shahine entered the principal's office, she found him sitting behind his desk with a wide smile on his face. "You'll never guess what I discovered this week. I learned that the son of the elder of your church attends school on Saturday! Why can't you?"

Surprised by this question, Shahine sighed deeply. What could she say? The choices of the elder and his son made it very difficult for her. Taking a deep breath, she replied, "I can't speak for the church elder or for his son or for what they do or don't do. What I can say is that I have to follow my own conscience and do what the Bible says I cannot follow people."

The principal exploded, "You're a very foolish girl!" For the rest of the day, Shahine didn't feel very happy, but the principal's outburst didn't alter her beliefs.

When the next Monday rolled around, the principal asked to speak with her parents. After school, Shahine told her father about the problem, asking, "Should I ask Mother to go?"

"No," her father replied. "I'll go talk with the principal for you."

"Thank you!" Shahine exclaimed, thinking it would be good for her Armenian father to explain her Adventist beliefs.

The next day Shahine's father went to school with her and paid a visit to the principal's office. Her father explained to him what his wife and daughter believed.

Finally, her graduation day neared. In Turkey, government officials wrote the final exam and determined on what day it would be given. All the students had to pass the government exam to graduate from high school. Knowing that the exam could be given on any day of the week, Shahine, filled with trepidation, scanned the board where information about the government exam was posted, hoping that it wouldn't be administered on a Saturday.

To her chagrin, she discovered that two of her exams were scheduled for Saturday.

That meant that she couldn't graduate that year. Feeling downhearted, she consoled herself that she could always repeat her senior year and hope the exams would be scheduled on another day the following school year. But that was little consolation, so she tried to put it out of her mind.

On the Friday before her final exam, the principal called her into his office and said, "Your exam is scheduled for tomorrow."

"I know," Shahine replied.

"You know that if you want to graduate, you must take the exam."

"I know," replied Shahine. A lump caught in her throat as she thought about what the principal would say next.

"Shahine, you absolutely *have to* take that exam! I *order* you to!"

"I won't be attending the exam," Shahine managed to say. "I'll be in church."

"I knew you'd say that," the principal replied. "Tell me, Shahine," he looked her in the eye, "do you want to graduate?"

"It means a lot to me. I want to graduate so much!" she exclaimed.

"I thought so," the principal said. "So I could make an arrangement with you. It would be a secret arrangement allowing you to take the exam, and no one would need to know about it."

"I don't want to compromise," Shahine explained. "I won't take the exam. Even in secret."

"You know that means you won't graduate." The principal was incredulous.

"I *still* won't take the exam, even if it means I can't graduate." Outwardly Shahine sounded bold, but inwardly, her heart was breaking.

That night she went home feeling terrible. She couldn't eat or take part in any of the regular family activities. As the family celebrated Friday night worship, she sat there but got very little out of it. She felt only a little better when she went up to her room to get ready for bed. As she lay, trying to sleep, a Bible text came to mind. *"All things work together for good to them that love God"* [Romans 8:28, KJV].

She thought, *I can't believe how that Bible promise can apply to me. I'm going to miss my exam tomorrow, so I'm not going to graduate! How can that work out for good because I love God?*

The next day she attended church, but barely listened to the services. *"Psst,"* someone whispered, tapping Shahine on the shoulder.

With a distant expression on her face, Shahine turned to see what they wanted and nodded slightly. "There's someone back there who wants to speak with you," the church member whispered. Craning her neck, Shahine peered over the church members sitting behind her, then noticed a schoolgirl in uniform.

"Why don't you see what that girl wants?" The church member whispered, glancing toward the schoolgirl. Puzzled, Shahine wondered who would want to talk with her at this time.

Remembering her manners, Shahine rose from her seat and quietly tiptoed outside.

To her surprise, it was one of her classmates. Shahine asked, "What are *you* doing here? Aren't you supposed to be sitting in the exam?"

"Yes, I am," the schoolgirl replied. "What're *you* doing here? You're supposed to be in the exam also."

Shahine told the girl, "I'm not going to take the exam because it's Sabbath."

"Did you forget that the principal made a secret arrangement? You can come with me, and I'll take you to the room where you can take the exam in secret. After you're finished, I'll take you back before church is over. Nobody will know."

Turning from her classmate, Shahine thought to herself, *So nobody will know, huh? Is that true? Let's see,* she mused. *The principal will know and you'll know. How many people will you tell? I'll know and God will know. That means at least four will know.* Looking her classmate in the eye, she said, "You shouldn't have come. I'm not going to take the exam today. I know that will make me flunk the class. But I won't take an exam on the Sabbath. To paraphrase Queen Esther, if it means I can't graduate, then I can't graduate!"

With that, her classmate left, and Shahine returned to her seat in church.

If it had been difficult for her to listen to the service before her classmate arrived, it was absolutely impossible now. All she could do was worry about not being able to graduate. A text flashed across her mind, *"All things work together for good to them that love God,"* but she tried to shut it from her consciousness. As the pastor preached, Shahine reasoned to herself, *All things include tests and that's not working together right now with this person who loves God, or she wouldn't be trying to spend time with Him in His holy house. I'm failing a test! Certainly all things do* not *work together for good to* me *who loves God. Why can't I get that text out of my mind? Isn't there a better one?*

Church ended. Dazed and confused, Shahine soon found herself at home, eating with her family. The rest of the day eventually passed, and the next thing she knew, it was Monday and she was back in school.

As usual, when she arrived at her desk, she found a note from the principal, saying he wanted to see her. Of course, she didn't want to see the principal. *It won't do any good,* she thought. *All he'll do is scold me and call me a silly girl for not taking advantage of his plan to help me take the test. Then he'll taunt me because I won't be able to graduate. Isn't it bad enough that I'll have to spend another year in school with that principal?* After Shahine calmed down, she reminded herself that he was the principal and that she should respect him, even though she didn't really want to see him. Slowly and reluctantly, she headed for the principal's office.

When she entered, the principal said, "You'd better sit down. I don't know if you can take what I'm going to say standing up. So, please sit."

Dutifully, Shahine obeyed.

"The God you worship just performed a miracle! I can't believe what just happened!" he exclaimed.

Shahine was puzzled. It wasn't what she'd expected to hear.

The principal continued. "I was pretty sure that you wouldn't come to take the test on Saturday, so I tried the impossible for you. I applied to the government, requesting that you be allowed to take the exam at another time—and a miracle happened." The principal seemed as jolly as a schoolboy. "I can't believe it! The letter arrived this morning from the government. It says you may take the exam at another time. Shahine, are you ready for your exam?"

"Yes!" Shahine exclaimed.

"Good! The government said you could take it Monday afternoon. That's today!" The principal paused, then asked with concern, "Do you think you could sit for the exam this afternoon?"

"Certainly," exclaimed Shahine. "Oh, thank you for everything!" She repressed the urge to jump from her chair and leap for joy.

Shahine took the exam that afternoon and passed with a very respectable score. How proud she was to be able to graduate with her class.

\* \* \* \* \*

After she received her diploma, Shahine decided she didn't want to attend other schools in Turkey. Middle East College in Lebanon had just become a coed institution, so Shahine became one of the first young women to attend Middle East College.

Not long after she'd settled into her new life as a freshman in college, she received a letter from her mother, saying, "You would've loved to have attended church this week. We had a baptism. She was a widow who gave her testimony before being baptized. You'd be interested in her story. She told the congregation that her husband had been a principal. 'Often he came home from school and related stories about a very stubborn girl who skipped school every Saturday. At first my husband thought her lazy. He'd describe her as stubborn and foolish and told me how extremely difficult she was.

" 'Then things changed. He began sharing with me her beliefs. He marveled that, unlike other Christians, she seemed to practice what she believed.' "

The letter continued. " 'Then came the big test. The government had placed the final test on Saturday, and my husband wondered how badly she wanted to graduate. Would she keep the Sabbath if it meant failing her final year? Then he shared his plan. He was so certain the government would do nothing to accommodate her that he thought this was the perfect opportunity to set up a secret exam—to learn for certain whether she really would keep the Sabbath. As the day of the exam neared, my husband felt sure that she might go along with his idea, despite the fact that she'd vowed to attend church on the day of the test.

" 'Then the day of the test arrived, and he related how he'd sent a schoolgirl to escort her to the room he'd set up for her to take the test secretly, but she'd kept her God's Sabbath to her own hurt.' "

Tears trickled down Shahine's face as she read that when this man had told his wife about how that schoolgirl's God had performed a miracle for her, the wife wanted to know more about her God. She began taking Bible studies and ended her testimony by saying, " 'It's because Shahine faithfully kept the Sabbath that I'm here being baptized today.' "

When she finished reading the letter, Shahine couldn't help thinking to herself, *What if I had faltered on that Sabbath of the exam?* If she'd taken the secret exam, she'd have failed the principal's test of her integrity. By standing firm that day, she'd allowed God to reveal His power to solve the impossible. Together they had passed two tests!

She thanked God for giving her the strength to stand up for what she believed, no matter how much she'd been ridiculed. If you were to ask her today, she'd say she's certain that no matter how bad it may seem at the moment, "All things really *do* work out for good to people who love God!"

# Andre and the Ambulance

**F**rench boys, when they reach a certain age, are expected to serve two years in the military. Andre wasn't looking forward to his tour of duty for two reasons. First, he was afraid he'd have to leave his home; and second, he feared he'd have difficulty keeping the Sabbath.

One day the dreaded letter arrived. After delaying almost to the deadline, Andre filled out the form and took it to the address where he was to report for his military assignment. Andre sat down with the officer on duty and answered his questions. The interview ended almost as quickly as it had begun. The officer rose and shook hands with Andre, who looked the recruiter in the eye and said, "Please assign me somewhere near my home."

The officer's face was difficult to read as he replied, "We'll do what we can."

Andre walked out the door. *At least,* he reasoned, *my request hasn't been denied outright.* He hoped for the best.

But when the letter announcing his assignment arrived, Andre didn't want to open it. After letting it lie on the table for a while, he tore it open and read the contents. To his dismay, he discovered he had been assigned to French Guiana, far across the Atlantic Ocean, which was obviously not near his home. *This makes no sense to me,* he thought. *The officer said he would do what he could!* Then Andre gave the matter over to the Lord, trusting that God knew what was best.

When he arrived in French Guiana, Andre found that it was nothing like France. He immediately hated the hot, tropical jungle.

Awakening early one morning, he joined his unit outside. "Line up!" shouted the sergeant, strutting around the men, eyeing them. "Attention!"

The men stood at attention. Andre was uncertain whether he should look straight ahead or keep his eyes on the sergeant. He decided to use his peripheral vision to watch the sergeant.

Suddenly, the sergeant stopped in front of the private standing next to Andre. "Didn't I say, 'Stand at attention'?"

"Something like that," the soldier mumbled sheepishly and looked down at the ground.

"What did you say?"

The soldier squirmed but spoke more clearly. "I said, 'You said something like that.' "

"Where are your manners, boy? When I speak to you, you're to answer, 'Yes, sir!' or 'No, sir!' " The sergeant bent down so that his hat touched the soldier's head. "Are you listening to me?"

"Of course," he replied.

"I can't hear you. Say, 'Yes, sir.' "

"Yes, sir!"

"Louder!" The sergeant lifted the soldier's chin.

"Yes, sir!" he shouted.

"That's better. Suck in your gut and stand at attention." He poked the soldier in the stomach.

"Yes, sir!" he shouted and stiffened.

"What's your name, boy? You got a name?"

"Pierre, sir!"

"Pierre?"

"Yes, sir!"

The sergeant glared at Pierre and sneered, "Tell me something about yourself, Pierre."

"I have a tendency to keep the Sabbath because I'm a Seventh-day Adventist."

The officer raised his eyebrows in bewilderment. Andre must have smiled when the soldier said, "Tendency to keep the Sabbath," because the sergeant turned on Andre. "Wipe that smirk off your face, Private!"

"Yes, sir." Andre found that no matter how hard he tried, it was difficult to keep a straight face.

"Is he jiving me, boy?" The sergeant asked Andre about Pierre.

"No, sir!" Andre couldn't get the idea of having a tendency to be a Sabbath keeping Seventh-day Adventist out of his head. He tried to curl his lips downward, but failed.

"What's so funny, boy?"

"I'm sorry, sir!" Andre shouted.

"I think you know something I need to know." The sergeant now eyeballed Andre.

"What's that, sir?"

"Do you know what he's talking about?"

"I do, sir!" Andre saluted.

The sergeant stood squarely in front of Andre and bent his face within inches of Andre's nose. "I thought so, soldier. Talk!"

"My name is Andre and unlike my friend here," Andre motioned by tipping his head toward Pierre, who smiled in nervous recognition, "I don't have a 'tendency' to keep the Sabbath. I definitely am a Seventh-day Adventist, and I definitely do make the seventh-day Sabbath a day of rest to attend church, worship God, and read my Bible."

A confused look clouded the sergeant's face. "I've never heard of 'Several-date Adventurers' before. Now I've heard the word twice in one day! What the devil are you talking about, boy?"

"Begging your pardon, sir," Andre clicked his heels politely. "The words you heard, sir, were 'Seventh-day Adventist.' "

"What is a Seventh-day Adventist?"

Andre smiled. He knew he'd have to talk about his beliefs. Better to do it sooner than later. "We're Sabbath keepers, but we're not Jews. Seventh-day Adventists are members of a Christian denomination that follows the Bible."

"We're all Catholic here," the sergeant sneered. "What do you little heretics believe?"

"We're Adventists because we love Jesus so much we look forward to His soon return, sir."

The sergeant loudly interrupted. "And the seventh-day part? Explain that!"

Without missing a beat, Andre continued, "Sir, we worship on the seventh-day Sabbath, which is Saturday, as indicated in the fourth commandment. We may work six days a week, but on the seventh day, we do no work, sir. Instead, we spend the time in worship, Bible study, and prayer."

"You're in the army now."

"Yes, sir." Andre shouted. "I will not be reporting for duty on Sabbath."

"Did I hear you right?"

"That's right. I'll be reading my Bible and praying on Sabbath."

The officer's eyes narrowed to angry slits. "Do you mean that if you're given an assignment, or if you're needed on Saturday, you won't report for duty?"

"That's right, sir."

The sergeant lifted Andre's chin, forcing him to look up into his eyes. "I prefer soldiers with no tendency toward Christian practices. There's no room for religion in foxholes."

"I understand, sir."

"Do you really think you'll get Sabbath off in the army?"

"I do, sir." Andre spoke firmly. "Upon request, sir. Through proper channels."

The sergeant assumed a condescending tone. "Let me tell you how things work in the army, boy. You'll do what you're told when you're told, because the army's all about discipline and doing your duty."

"I understand. I *will* do what I'm told. I *will* be disciplined, but I *will* not report for duty on Sabbath, sir!"

The officer exploded. "If you don't report for duty, I'll personally see to it that you suffer. You'll spend time in prison for insubordination. Do we understand each other?"

"Yes, sir." Andre tipped his head respectfully. "You should do your duty, as should I, but I won't report for duty on the Sabbath."

The sergeant stormed off, uttering a stream of obscenities. "Try me! You'll regret it until you learn your lesson."

Andre was as good as his word. Every Friday he filled out the proper forms requesting Sabbath off to read his Bible and pray. Fortunately, he was assigned to the dispensary, where he worked as a medic. His immediate supervisor, a corporal, habitually granted permission for him to have Sabbath free to worship because he was more dependable than any of the other medics.

His real test came when his unit was given the honor of protecting the president of the country. It was an enviable assignment, coveted by all the soldiers. Andre's unit felt privileged to be chosen. Everyone, including Andre, was excited about the challenge of keeping the president safe. But when Andre discovered that part of the assignment would require duty on the Sabbath, he informed his superior officers that he wouldn't report for duty that day.

People thought he was crazy. "Soldiers dream of such an assignment, but you're quibbling over a day of worship," they criticized.

Andre said that he understood. "I'll happily serve on all the other days, but I *won't* report for duty on Sabbath."

His superiors grew angry. "You'll be sentenced to three weeks in prison for disobedience."

Andre swallowed hard, knowing that prisons in French Guiana were not places one wanted to go. Then he replied, "I'm willing to go to prison if that's what I must do to keep God's day holy."

Slamming his fist against the desktop, his superior declared, "You're just guarding the president. Couldn't you make an exception rather than go to prison?"

Andre replied, "I've read Bible stories where God delivered people from prison, sir."

"You're impossible!" the officer roared.

"God can release me from jail as he did Peter and Paul, sir."

The superior officer shook his head. "Be reasonable, Andre."

"God could send His angel, or He could cause an earthquake to unlock the doors and set me free," Andre said boldly. "Even if He doesn't, I won't report for duty on Sabbath."

Seeing that Andre was unfazed by anything he'd said, the officer sighed. "All right, I'll see what I can do—but no promises."

"Thank you, sir." Andre saluted.

Shaking his head, the bewildered officer added, "If you weren't such a good worker, Andre, I'd call you crazy and lazy."

Seeing that he was dismissed, Andre returned to his barracks and awaited his fate. It wasn't long before he learned that his request had been denied. His arrest and prison term were imminent.

As he packed his things, he prayed, reminding God of the story of Peter. "God, I'll be generous. I'll give You two days to get me released from that terrible prison."

But God had other plans of which Andre did not know. When he didn't show up for duty on Sabbath, he expected to be arrested that morning, but nobody banged on his door.

That night when he went to bed, he was certain he'd be arrested Sunday morning. But nobody came to take him to prison. *Perhaps they didn't come because it was the weekend. Surely they'll come for me on the third day, Monday,* he thought.

Monday was uneventful. Nothing happened.

Andre grew curious, so he talked to his friends who sat in on important meetings. "What's going on?" he asked. "Why haven't I been arrested?"

They promised to discover the answer. It wasn't long before they returned. "What have you learned?" he asked eagerly.

One informant told Andre that the corporal, his immediate supervisor in the medical dispensary, had gone to the court and informed the magistrates. The informant changed his voice to a deeper tone to sound more like an older man. "If Andre is placed in prison, the medical clinic would fall apart in his absence."

"He said that!" Andre exclaimed, happy that his supervisor appreciated him.

"Yes. He further explained that you're different from the other medics."

"How so?" Andre asked curiously.

"The corporal said the others just put in their time, but when evening comes, they tell Andre to cover for them. They slip out the back door, jump over the fence, and go to bars, or seek out prostitutes, leaving Andre to do all the work for them."

"I've never reported on any of them. How does he know?" Andre marveled aloud.

His informant shrugged, "I dunno. He somehow knows you remain on duty and do the work for all of them. Perhaps he has informants like you do." They smiled at each other knowingly. Everyone had informants in French Guiana.

Andre asked, "Do you know the court verdict?"

His informant nodded. "The court reluctantly agreed not to put you in prison, but it ruled that if you refuse a second time, you won't be granted clemency."

Andre thanked his informant and, with a lighter heart, returned to work in the clinic.

All went well for a time.

But after a while, Andre's unit was again selected to perform privileged guard duty. Only this time, instead of protecting the president, it was the vice president of the nation. Again Andre said he wouldn't report for duty on Sabbath.

This time the court sentenced him to two weeks' imprisonment.

Again Andre awaited arrest on Saturday, but no one came. Again he learned from his informants that the corporal had pleaded his case, praising his work in the clinic. Soon he was back serving the sick without ever having seen the inside of prison walls.

Not long after that, the authorities granted him Sabbaths off every week. Every Saturday he changed out of uniform into a suit to walk down the streets to the nearest church.

Just when he thought his worries were over, one Sabbath morning he heard the siren of an ambulance coming toward his barracks. When it stopped in front of his door, the driver leaned over, rolled down the window, and said, "Get in, Andre."

"There must be some mistake," Andre protested, showing his papers authorizing him to leave the base. "I was granted permission to attend church. Did somebody forget this is my Sabbath?"

The driver chuckled good-naturedly at Andre's confusion. "There's no mistake. I've been ordered to *drive* you to your destination."

"I'm not going to the clinic," Andre insisted, holding out the papers. "Let me go to church to worship. At this rate, I'll be late if I don't hurry."

"Hop in, Andre," the driver urged again.

"Into an ambulance?" Andre asked as he shook his head. "These vehicles are for emergencies."

"What are the roads like on Sabbath morning?" The driver wore a broad smile. "Is the traffic usually pretty heavy?"

Andre admitted it usually was.

"Didn't I hear you say that you're almost late?"

Andre agreed.

"Wouldn't it be faster if you let me take you to church in my ambulance?" The driver's eyes twinkled mischievously. "Everyone would get out of your way, and you'd be in church in no time."

"Do you mean you're going to take me to church in an *ambulance*?"

"I'm your chauffeur, Andre." The driver opened the ambulance door from the inside. "My orders are to escort you to the church. Hop in!"

Andre now happily obliged. Once outside the army camp, the driver turned on the siren. Andre watched in amazement as the pedestrians, bicycles, pushcarts, and motorcars parted like the Red Sea to allow them to pass. At this rate, he thought, he'd arrive at church early. "What happens after the service?" he asked.

"I'll take you back," the driver grinned.

"How will you know when the service is over? Should I call?"

"No need," the driver replied. "I'll be sitting out here, waiting for you during the service; then I'll drive you back to your barracks."

After the service, the ambulance, with its siren blaring, drove him through the crowds back to the army camp. Indeed, for the rest of his two-year tour of duty, every Sabbath he rode to church in the army ambulance.

Reflecting back on those days, Andre marvels at how God helped him solve his problems in the military. He'd learned much about God's faithfulness, and his faith grew.

But the story ended quite differently for the soldier who'd announced that he "had a tendency" to be a Sabbath keeping Seventh-day Adventist. Not long afterward, he was commanded to appear for duty on Sabbath. Sadly, he failed the test of lovingly obeying God's law. Never was he allowed to have the day off. Soon he was working every Sabbath.

Andre was thankful that he'd announced he was *definitely* a Seventh-day Adventist and had stood firm in his refusal to work on Sabbath. He knows that God will help anyone who really wants to follow his conscience.

# Did the Pastor Work for the KGB?

## Part 1: Mondays in the Principal's Office

When Irina was growing up in the Union of Soviet Socialist Republics (USSR), known informally as the Soviet Union, her grandmother was in prison. Everyone in the family knew why.

She'd been traveling all over the country telling people about her love for Jesus. The government didn't mind her being a Christian—as long as she stayed at home on the weekdays, attended church on the weekends, and didn't share her faith with anyone who wasn't a Christian. But Irina's grandmother thought differently. She shared her love of Jesus with everyone, so the government had arrested her and thrown her into prison.

Irina knew what her grandmother was doing in prison—witnessing.

She was happy to be there because no one could arrest her there! How could they? She was already in prison, so she was free to witness to all who wanted to hear about Jesus.

When Irina turned seven, she had to attend school. Going to school in the USSR wasn't easy because students were required to attend classes six days a week, from Monday to Saturday. Irina and her family didn't call the seventh day of the week Saturday; they called it the Sabbath. Every Sabbath her parents took her to church. Irina liked to go to church on Sabbath and learn more about Jesus and other Bible heroes.

On the Friday of Irina's first week in school, her parents said, "If you want to attend church tomorrow, you may." There was no mention of school.

The next day Irina went to church, not to school.

However, on Sunday, her parents took her aside and asked, "What will you say tomorrow when your principal asks why you weren't in school yesterday?"

"I don't know," Irina said.

"Will you say your parents wanted you to go to church?"

"Yes, Mommy." Irina smiled sweetly.

"No!" Mommy and Daddy said. "You mustn't say that."

"Why not?" Irina asked.

Her parents bent closer to her. "Do you want your mommy and daddy to go to prison?"

"No!" Irina shook her head fearfully.

"If you say it was our idea, you'd become an orphan," Daddy replied.

"How do you know?" Irina asked suspiciously.

Mommy's face looked sad. "What do you think happened to your mommy when your grandmother was arrested?"

Irina thought for a moment, then shook her head. "I don't know."

"All right," Mother smiled. "Sit down." Irina obeyed. Her parents sat beside her. "When your grandmother was arrested, I was sixteen. Your uncle Boris ran away. He couldn't take being considered a child of a thought criminal and a counterrevolutionary. He went back to the life he'd had before—I guess." Her voice trailed off as she gazed into the distance. "We have no idea whether he's alive or dead." Mommy looked sad. "But then he was adopted."

"What happened to my other uncle and my auntie?" Irina wanted to know.

"Your uncle Vladimir was a teenager, and your auntie Nadia was only six—just about your age. The four of us were essentially orphans."

"What's an orphan?" Irina asked.

"An orphan is someone whose mother and father have died," Mommy answered.

"But your mother wasn't dead," Irina stated. "She's still in prison today."

"Yes, you're right," her mother replied. "But when she went to prison, she was as good as dead."

"Why?"

"Because she wasn't around to take care of us, and we had nobody else to be our mommy and daddy." Mommy's voice sounded sad.

"Who took care of you?"

"No one really," Mommy had tears in her eyes. "Some of the church members let us stay with them. After a few months, they looked through our house and told us we should give them something for their care. We agreed. They asked for our piano and organ, and we let them carry them away. A few weeks later, they announced they'd found another family willing to take us in. The cycle repeated itself many times. Each time the church members took something. We got poorer and poorer until we feared we'd have nothing left." Mommy wiped her eyes. "Then we wondered, 'Who will take care of us?' The pressure was too much for your uncle Vladimir. He stopped being a Christian. He's an atheist now. Your auntie Nadia and I, on the other hand, are still Christians, and we never went to school on Sabbath because we wanted to honor your grandmother who was witnessing in prison."

Irina sat thinking about Mommy's story.

"We'll coach you, Irina. We'll ask questions the principal will ask." Mommy put her arm around Irina and smiled, "Don't worry, we'll tell you how to answer."

"Do you want me to lie?" Irina looked worried.

"No, dearie, you won't be lying," Mommy reassured Irina. "You'll just give answers that won't get us into trouble; besides, don't forget, I asked you whether you wanted to go to church on Sabbath and you said, 'Yes.' "

"How do you know what questions the principal will ask, Mommy?"

"Trust us!" Mommy and Daddy said in unison. Mother continued, "Remember, we told you that Auntie Nadia and I never went to school on Sabbath?"

Irina nodded.

"Do you think we got called into the principal's office?"

"Yes, Mommy," Irina said.

"You're right, Irina. The principal asked us many questions—hard questions. Do you think they were easy?"

Irina's eyes grew big. "No, Mommy."

"You're right; they weren't. With your grandma in prison, we didn't have anyone to coach us; however, God helped us. With His wisdom, we came up with good answers." Mother smiled lovingly. "Your principal will likely ask the same questions ours did. We remember all of his questions as if it happened yesterday. Oh, in case you wondered, we also remember our answers. So I think we can help you."

"OK, Mommy." Irina requested her mommy to ask questions she thought the principal would ask. "Teach me what to say."

So they asked her, "Why weren't you in school Saturday?"

"I was in church," Irina answered.

"You're supposed to be in school, not in church!" her parents roared. "Was it your parents' idea?"

Irina opened her mouth to say Yes, but her mommy stopped her. "Now here you say, 'No! It was my idea.' And stick to that. Don't say anything else. If you don't say it was your idea, your parents will get arrested, do you understand?"

Wide-eyed, Irina nodded. "You've got to repeat this answer until you know it in your sleep." So they practiced. They asked her again and again until she gave all the honest answers that her parents had taught her.

The next day when Irina went to school, she found that the answers that she had practiced weren't helpful. The principal didn't ask her any questions at all. Instead, he called her "anti-party," and a "troublemaker." In assembly, the principal talked about her by name in front of all her classmates. "Irina thinks she doesn't have to obey school rules," he asserted. "She's lazy and skips class. She's a problem student—a bad girl—probably with a troubled home life." Poor Irina wanted to crawl under her chair, but the space was too small. Instead, she slumped far down in her chair, hoping she could become invisible

It seemed that everyone was staring at her. The principal pointed an accusing finger at her, demanding that she see him in his office after assembly. She slumped further in her chair, trembling all over. Despite the fact that she knew all the answers to the questions she'd hear, she dreaded the time when she'd meet the principal. While she was prepared intellectually, she wasn't ready emotionally.

Once Irina was inside his office, her hands shook visibly and her voice was barely audible.

"Why didn't you come to school Saturday?" the principal began predictably. As he continued ranting, his voice became more intimidating. "Don't you know it's against the rules to play hooky? We can't tolerate truancy. Don't skip classes! You must come to school every day from Monday through Saturday!" He told her she'd get behind in her lessons. "Now tell me," his voice boomed, making Irina feel more scared. "Why weren't you in school on Saturday?"

In a faint, trembling voice, Irina replied, "Because I went to church on Sabbath."

"Why did you go to church?"

She told him.

"Was it your parents' idea?"

"No, it was my idea."

"Did they make you go?"

"No, it was my idea," she stammered.

He raved on and on, telling her to be on time for school every day. "Don't attend church next week!" he ordered. Then he let her go.

The next Saturday, she again attended church with her parents. When the pastor stepped to the pulpit, he began his sermon with a shocking statement: "I don't want to see any children in church. If you parents don't send your children to school, the government will close this church. Then we won't have a house of worship. I'm so serious about this," the pastor asserted, "that I'm sending my own son to school."

On Sunday Irina's parents again coached her. "Irina, what are you going to say when the principal asks you about the pastor's son?"

"Mommy," Irina asked, "why is the pastor sending his son to school on the Sabbath?"

"He's probably connected with the secret police called the KGB. He may be a spy, or at least a collaborator, working with the Communist government."

Irina's mouth dropped in shock. "Our *pastor*? Working with the Communists?" she asked. "But why?"

"We suspect our atheist government has promised him *something*— most likely keeping his job—if he persuades his church members to send their kids to school on Sabbath."

"And our pastor agreed to that?" Irina could hardly believe her ears.

"So it seems." Her mother shrugged. "People have to follow their own conscience."

"Should I tell the principal our pastor is KGB?" Irina asked.

"I think I can give you a better answer," Mommy smiled. "You say, 'I cannot speak about what the pastor's son is doing, or why he comes to school instead of going to church with his father. I must follow my conscience.' " So they practiced it.

But when she went to school on Monday and sat in her seat in the assembly hall, the principal again singled her out for ridicule and scorn. He ranted and raved about how delinquent she was. Again Irina wished she could hide. Again she slumped down as far as she could, almost sliding off her chair. Try as she might, she was still the center of unwanted attention. If only the principal would stop talking about her. Inwardly, she screamed, *Talk about something else!* Soon she saw his finger pointing at her, as if no one knew where she was. "Irina," he demanded, "see me in my office immediately after assembly."

Irina didn't want to see him again even though she'd practiced what to say. She wasn't quite eight years old and was very frightened, but she knew she needed to cooperate with the principal wherever she could. Reluctantly, she dragged her feet to the principal's door and knocked.

He opened it, invited her in, and ordered her to sit across from his desk. "You know your pastor sends his son to school on Saturday, so I don't think you need to be in church that day. Come to school next week! Would you like me to bring your pastor to explain to you that you don't need to attend church on Sabbath?"

In a faint, trembling voice that was almost inaudible, Irina remembered what she'd rehearsed. "I can't speak for the pastor or for his son.

All I can follow is my conscience. My conscience says that I need to be in church on Sabbath because I want to worship my God and spend the whole day with Him."

The principal scolded her. Irina felt smaller with each angry word. Slumping before the principal and trembling from head to foot, she hung her head as she spoke her prepared lines, her voice nervous and her hands shaky. Eventually, the principal calmed down and let her go. "Don't go to church next week!" he admonished as she left.

The next Sabbath, when she arrived in church, most of the other parents looked sideways at her—and at her parents. "Who do you think you are?" they asked. "Do you think you're holier than we are? Do you want to make us look bad? You heard the pastor tell us last week to send our children to school. We complied. Do you want the government to close down our church? If so, the blame will fall on *you*!"

"We don't want the church to close," Irina's parents replied. "But we have to follow our beliefs. We don't know how Irina can keep the Sabbath holy while studying in school."

As long as Irina ignored the nasty looks and snide remarks from some of the members, she really enjoyed the church services. She even delighted in the day. It was exciting to learn things on Sabbath in church—things she wouldn't learn in school. Fortunately, she wasn't the only child attending church. Irina loved spending time with the handful of children who kept the Sabbath and didn't study in school that day.

Indeed, Sabbath was a wonderful day for her—until Monday came along. She dreaded being ridiculed by her principal in assembly and later by her fellow students. On Monday, she needed to remember the replies her parents had taught her. Every time she sat in the principal's office she trembled, but her faint voice repeated the answers until the principal, in exasperation, let her go.

No matter how hard it was for her, Irina never attended school on Sabbath throughout all her days in elementary school. When she entered high school, something unexpected happened.

One of her classmates named Natasha began attending church on Sabbath. When Natasha had been in elementary school, her parents had followed the pastor's advice and sent her to school, but after watching Irina, she had decided she wasn't keeping the Sabbath when she sat in class.

It was difficult for Natasha because she hadn't been attending church on Saturday for so many years. The principal asked her many times, "Why have you changed? You could attend school on Saturday before; why does it bother your conscience now?" He nearly exploded when Natasha said, "I changed my mind after watching Irina's example."

Natasha had an additional problem Irina didn't have. Irina was a straight-A student. She could ask a friend for the class assignments given on Saturday, work on them on Sunday, and get a good grade. It was different for Natasha. When she skipped school on Saturday to attend church, she had difficulty making up her homework on Sunday. Already struggling to maintain a B average before she'd decided to follow her conscience, her grades now plummeted from Bs to Cs in some classes.

The principal was quick to notice the change and made sure she never forgot it. He told everyone at assembly, "Natasha is only hurting herself by not attending school and following the rules!"

Hard as it was for her, she persisted. Eventually, the students and school officials stopped harassing her. They continued calling her into the office, but they seemed to understand that she meant what she said.

When graduation day came, both Irina and Natasha were allowed to march. Irina thinks the greatest blessing was that her refusal to go to school on the Sabbath helped a fellow classmate follow her example. Both girls praised God for their experience in school because they felt that it helped them grow in their Christian experience.

## Part 2: The KGB Files Opened

Irina noticed that the pastor's son, who'd attended classes on Saturday, had been accepted into the best program in a top-ranking college. It was the same story for all the children of church members who'd been in school when they should've been in church. They, too, had been granted interviews by the best colleges, and were allowed to study in the best programs the country offered. Yet Irina's mailbox remained empty. She and Natasha received no interviews to any colleges.

While Natasha's B average might explain her situation, Irina was an A student, so she suspected something was amiss.

The girls requested to look at their dossiers and found them to be revealing. They said that in school the girls were very good, but that they had problems at home. Both girls knew that they had *not* lived in troubled families. Nowhere did their dossiers mention that their families were Christian. "Problems at home" may have been a code term for students who practiced their religion.

Irina didn't give up though. Eventually, due to her good grades, her efforts were rewarded; the Soviet Union permitted her to study secretarial science in a second-tier university. But when she finished school and began to work, she discovered the pay was bad, and life was hard.

However, God blessed Irina in an unexpected way. The Soviet Union broke up and was reborn, for the most part, as Russia. With the fall of Communism, the world as Irina had known it ended. Religious freedom was granted, and an Adventist Theological Seminary was built near Moscow. After seeing Irina's grades and her financial situation, someone offered to sponsor her. The anonymous benefactor promised to pay her entire tuition at the seminary. Irina took coursework in the translation of biblical languages.

Not long after she began classes at the seminary, she met a young man named Sasha, who, as a boy, had shared similar struggles in his school life. He, too, had ignored his pastor's advice and had worshiped in church instead of attending classes on Sabbath. Because of their shared experiences and convictions, they felt they had much in common. Soon Sasha became Irina's boyfriend.

One day Sasha ran up to her, beaming with excitement. "Did you hear the news about the KGB?" he asked.

"Doesn't the KGB try to keep out of the news?" Irina replied suspiciously. "I thought they were supposed to keep secrets, not broadcast them."

"That's the news!" Sasha exclaimed. "The KGB is opening its secret files to the public."

"Incredible! So what does that mean?" Irina had a funny feeling about his information. "How do you know this?"

"Oh, it was announced that anyone can read the files. Irina, at last we can get the truth."

"The truth?" Irina was again suspicious. "Does the KGB have the truth?"

"Yes and no. But you know what I mean, I think," her boyfriend explained. "We're talking about KGB records. We'll know the truth about who was collaborating with the KGB."

"Do you really want to know?" Irina asked.

"Yes," Sasha said. "When you and I were growing up, we were forced to be different from the others. We disobeyed our teachers and pastors who told us not to keep the Sabbath—and we suffered."

"And many of our pastors sent their children to school on Sabbath," Irina added.

"Look at those children today," Sasha said. "They get all the good jobs in the country—and even sometimes in the church. It's as if they were rewarded for breaking God's law."

"What do you have in mind?" Irina asked somewhat fearfully.

"There will be a meeting with all the pastors soon. I want to expose the pastors who collaborated with the Communists," her boyfriend said. "Those of us who were true to the Sabbath should be pastors now. Can we trust those who compromised with the KGB and told parents to send their children to school on Sabbath?"

"They did wrong," Irina admitted.

"Moscow's just a short train ride from here," Sasha said. "Look," he held out a piece of paper with a list on it. Irina looked and saw the names of pastors they both knew—pastors who'd sent their children to school on Sabbath. "I want to know the relationship, if any, these pastors had with the KGB. We have freedom now in Russia, and I want to exercise it."

"Shouldn't freedom come with responsibility?" Irina almost whispered. Apparently, Sasha didn't hear her, so instead she asked, "What do you plan to do?"

Sasha exclaimed, "I'll look up their files. When I return, I'll expose the collaborators and reform our church."

Irina knew that when her boyfriend wanted to do something, it was not her place to give her opinion or to say anything to discourage him. He learned best by doing, so she said, "It'll be interesting to learn what you discover. When do you plan on going?"

He told her. "Right away, so I'll get back before the meeting."

Off he went down to the station, where he bought his ticket.

When he arrived in Moscow, Sasha promptly headed for the old KGB building, walked up to the desk of the receptionist, and presented his list. "I'd like to see the files for these people."

The receptionist examined the list and indicated some names. "We can show you files for these."

"What about the others?" Sasha asked.

"They're not available," was the vague reply.

"But may I read the selected files?" Sasha tried to hide his disappointment that he couldn't read every file he wished.

"Certainly," the receptionist said without smiling. He shuffled off and later returned with a stack of folders. "You have to read them here. These can't leave the building."

"I understand," Sasha said as he received the papers. Eagerly, Sasha pored over the pages and soon discovered the information he wanted.

Returning to the receptionist, he asked, "May I copy some of these pages?"

"*Nyet,*" the receptionist replied harshly. "It's forbidden for you to copy them, but we can do it for you for a small fee."

Sasha asked the price and gave him the money. The receptionist ambled off for what seemed an inordinate amount of time. *Seventy years of*

*Soviet Socialist rule has certainly bled efficiency out of many a lowly bureaucrat,* Sasha concluded. Eventually, the receptionist returned. "Here are your copies," he intoned.

Eagerly grabbing them, Sasha thanked the receptionist, hastily departed the KGB building, and headed for the train station.

Standing on the platform awaiting his train to the seminary, he pondered how he would use his newfound treasure. *Information is power,* he gloated. *My information is irrefutable because it's recorded by none other than the Soviet Union's finest spies.*

The first person he visited back at the seminary was Irina. "I've got it!" he exclaimed.

"So you know forbidden fruit?"

Sasha beamed. "You could say that. I have proof about who was on the Lord's side and who worked with the KGB."

"Sounds so biblical," Irina thought aloud.

"Do you want to see the files?" he asked.

She did—but at the same time—she didn't. After a pause, she said, "Did you find out about my childhood pastor?"

"I did," Sasha said. "Your suspicions were right."

After leaving Irina, Sasha told his plan to people at the seminary. He would expose the pastors involved with the KGB in the next pastoral conference. Word of his trip to Moscow spread.

Naturally, many people disapproved of Sasha's visit to the KGB. Many pastors trembled when they learned of his intentions, fearing that they might now lose their jobs. All knew that the records in the KGB files contained information they didn't want shared.

Others felt jealous that the children of pastors who attended school on Sabbath now had enviable jobs in free Russia. Church members wanted to know that their pastors could be trusted. They wanted leaders who'd be true to their faith no matter what the consequences. They didn't want leaders who had compromised their beliefs to obtain a better education or to gain better jobs.

Regrettably, instead of confessing and making things right, the collaborating pastors got together out of fear and decided they should call a meeting to discuss the issue. Sasha welcomed the idea. He was there, with the files in hand.

After some discussion, he was given the podium. Looking over the pastors, he felt like Moses before the earth swallowed up Korah. Or was he Elijah when he stood before the people on Mount Carmel? Opening the folder, he began reading.

Suddenly, one of the leaders, seemingly still operating out of fear of the possible results rather than out of faithfulness to God, began loudly protesting, "This will split the church!"

Others chimed in, "You're too young to know what these pastors experienced!"

Looking up, Sasha parried, "I suffered because my pastor urged us schoolchildren to go to school, not church, on Sabbath." Searching the eyes of the pastors, he inquired, "Shouldn't my pastor have praised me for standing strong in tough times? Shouldn't he have encouraged me in church after I was scolded at school for worshiping on the Sabbath? You're not the only ones who suffered. All the children suffered. Did you think about that when you compromised with the KGB?" He continued reading, but was soon interrupted.

Still vainly seeking to justify their faithless actions, some shouted, "The Bible says we should follow the laws of the land because the rulers are the ministers of God."

Another cried out, "We did what we thought we *had* to do to keep the churches open." Another added, "We saved the church property by compromising."

"What makes you think God needs vacillating leaders?" Sasha asked. "To paraphrase a famous saying," he added, " 'If you don't stand for something, you'll compromise away everything.' "

"The government compromised with us when they saw we weren't stubborn," yelled some pastors, still trying to justify their weak-minded and faithless decisions. "Believe us," they added, "you have no idea how much the church gained by cooperating with the Communists."

"With all due respect," Sasha responded, "may I suggest that because you compromised, you'll never know what miracles God might have performed for you if you'd been bolder."

"You forget, young man, that the bold pastors lost their churches and served prison terms!" they retorted. "Our spirit was willing, but our flesh was weak," some lamely quipped.

No one could hear what Sasha was reading. The shouts grew louder, "You should have a forgiving spirit." Sadly, none of the compromisers had the holy boldness to confess their sinful failures.

Seeking to deceptively sidetrack Sasha, a leader yelled, "Consider carefully the spirit in which you make these accusations."

Contradicting the clear word of Jesus that spiritual leaders are to be known by their fruits, another shouted, "Who are you to judge us? Let God be the Judge."

Hearing the words "Who are you to judge us?" made Sasha stop. He'd just finished reading one file. Looking at the pastors, he saw how frightened some of them appeared. *Clearly the Holy Spirit still has work to do in their lives,* he thought. *Perhaps I've punished them enough by just bringing the files. Knowing I have access to their files must fill them with fear. Besides,* he concluded, *don't the Scriptures say, " 'Vengeance is Mine, I will repay,' says the Lord"?* (Romans 12:19, NKJV).

Sasha quietly placed the rest of his files back into his folder and smiled. "I'm not going to read anymore," he announced. He heard a collective sigh of relief.

Then he looked into his own heart and realized that, while he didn't regret addressing this problem, he had a problem himself. He resented the suffering he'd endured at the hand of his pastor, and the resentment was a sin that he needed to overcome. Taking a deep breath, he asserted, "I forgive you." Having said those words, he felt as though the pent-up hard feelings and resentments he'd harbored against his childhood pastor had rolled off his own back, crashed into the cross of Christ, and vanished. "The Soviet Union is gone," he continued. "We all live in a new world now—one with freedom we've never experienced before." Graciously, like the prophet Daniel, who, though he'd been loyal to God, took on the collective blame of Israel by including himself in their faults, Sasha added, "Let's thank God for this second chance, and sin no more."

With that, he turned and left the pulpit without his previous load of resentment.

# The Tale of
# Two Cockroaches

The Lutheran minister couldn't sleep. He'd just had an extraordinary dream that he thought must be important. In the dream, he'd seen a man come to him and sell him a book. He couldn't remember ever having seen the man before, nor could he remember the book; but he seemed certain that, when the time came, he'd recognize both the man and the book.

One day a man came to his house. The Lutheran minister recognized him as the man in his dream. Not surprisingly, the man was selling books, Christian books to be exact. The book the seller showed the minister was exactly the one he remembered seeing in his dream.

Naturally, he eagerly bought it and read it.

He found the book to be very spiritual, but one section of the book bothered him. It was the section that stated emphatically that the Lord's Day wasn't Sunday. The Lord's Day was the Sabbath, which was not on the first, but on the seventh day of the week.

He read the section again. It said that the first day was not the Sabbath. *This can't be right,* he thought to himself. *How can so many Christians worship on Sunday and be wrong?* He sat thinking, then answered his own question. *They can't be!*

He continued preaching on Sundays, but couldn't get the idea of Sabbath and Sunday out of his mind.

One night he tossed and turned. He couldn't stand the nagging question any longer. He picked up the book and, with all his might, hurled it into the wastebasket. Then he shouted, "That's the last of *you*! I hope I *never* see you or hear of your crazy ideas again." Thinking he could now get a good night's sleep, he returned to his bed. But he couldn't get the book's ideas out of his head.

Wearily, he dragged himself out of bed the next morning. Still unable to forget the Sabbath idea, he devised a plan to settle the matter once and for all. That night his wife saw him take two bowls, fill them with water, and set them on the kitchen table. He took two pieces of paper and wrote something on each of them.

"What are you doing?" she asked.

Then he told her everything—all about the dreams and the book and the Sabbath and how the question of which day to worship on was bothering him. "I feel certain that so many Christians couldn't be wrong."

"Then why are you so worried?" she asked.

"I've devised a test that I believe will put my mind at rest." The Lutheran minister smiled.

"Does it have something to do with these bowls filled with water?" His wife grinned knowingly. "And those two pieces of paper marked Sabbath and Sunday?"

"It does indeed." Her husband squirmed sheepishly. "Let me explain."

"Did you notice that these two bowls of water are empty?" her husband asked.

"Empty?" she asked, looking at the water in them. "What do you mean by 'empty'?"

"There's nothing in them but water," he explained. "And, more to the point," he added, "there's nothing in the water—nothing floating on or in or under the water. You see that?"

"What I see is two bowls of water, and there's nothing in the water," she confirmed.

"Good." He pointed. "Look. One bowl I've marked Sunday, and the other I've marked Sabbath."

"So I see," his wife said.

"Do you like cockroaches?" he asked.

"Who likes cockroaches?" she replied.

"I like them dead, don't you?" her husband said, as they laughed. "However, they're great survivors."

"What does this have to do with your bowls?" she asked.

"I want to put God to the test. I've prayed that He'll make clear to me which day is His. I asked that by daybreak tomorrow morning, I want one bowl to have only water in it and the other to have a dead cockroach floating on top of the water. The bowl with the dead cockroach is the real Lord's Day."

His wife grew excited about the idea. "It's a great test. You're a modern-day Gideon."

"And don't forget, we kill a cockroach too!" the minister exclaimed.

"That's like the dry fleece—an irrefutable sign from God and clear guidance for our future," his wife said.

"I think I'll sleep well tonight." The minister beamed.

That night both the minister and his wife slept soundly. But long before dawn, the minister became restless. He could hardly wait for sunrise to see how God had answered his prayer. But which bowl should he root for? *Is it for Sunday to be confirmed, or for the Sabbath to be proved?* He couldn't decide. All he knew was that he was willing to accept the verdict.

At the crack of dawn, the Lutheran minister got out of bed and hurried to the kitchen. His wife followed him. When he got there, he saw the bowls, still clearly marked, sitting on the table where he'd left them.

Holding his breath, he peered into the bowls. In the bowl marked "Sunday" was only water, but in the bowl marked "Sabbath," floating atop the water was not one, but *two* dead cockroaches.

The Lutheran preacher could contain himself no longer. He jumped up and down, shouting, "It's *not* Sunday! The *Sabbath* is the Lord's Day!"

Soon he was telling everyone who'd listen about his dreams, the two dead cockroaches floating in a bowl of water, and the book with Bible truths.

\* \* \* \* \*

Today, the minister no longer serves the Lutheran congregation; he's the pastor of a Seventh-day Adventist church in Africa.

To this day, he loves to tell the story of how he tested God and of the two cockroaches that God used to prove to him that the seventh-day Sabbath is the day on which God wants the human race to worship Him.

# The Man Who Prayed for His Captors' Success!

**H**ere's a story that many people may not realize happened on a Sabbath. It reveals a potentially surprising relationship between the Jews, the Romans, and the Christians. But mostly it tells of a man of character who was willing to remain firm though the world around him fell apart.

Let's go back two thousand years to the first centuries after Christ when Rome ruled the Mediterranean world and the emperors didn't know how to deal with a new "superstition": Christianity. *How can people worship a Man who'd been condemned as a criminal by the Romans and crucified between two thieves?* they marveled. People who believed in Christ were considered by the polytheistic Romans to be atheists because they worshiped only *one* God, and they were unwilling to worship all the other gods in the Roman pantheon.

What made the Romans most upset was that the Christians refused to worship the Caesars. For this reason, Christians were punished. If they wouldn't comply by burning incense to the emperor or by cursing Christ, they were taken to the Colosseum, beaten, tortured, and fed to lions, or burned at the stake.

Many of the Christians at that time lived in hiding, dwelling in underground burial chambers called catacombs. There they hid from the erratic persecution that came their way. The secrecy of their organization led to rumors that spread. Romans believed Christians were incestuous cannibals who craved human blood (actually, Christians were reported to drink the blood of Christ and eat of His flesh)—all the more reason to hunt them down and feed them to lions.

In the city of Smyrna, in modern-day Turkey, lived a patriarch named Polycarp. He was a disciple of John the Beloved, who'd been a disciple of Jesus. By the time of our story, Polycarp had become the bishop of the church at Smyrna. He was an old man who'd lived through many persecutions. In Polycarp's twilight years, the emperor Marcus Aurelius instigated another persecution.

The authorities captured a Christian named Germanicus and took him to the amphitheater, where he died in glorious bravery for Christ, becoming food for beasts. The crowd roared with excitement as they watched the fight and cried for more Christians, shouting, "Away with the atheists!" Someone in the crowd cried, "Fetch Polycarp—he's the leader of the Christians at Smyrna!"

The crowd seated in the arena went wild. "Polycarp! Polycarp! We want Polycarp!" they yelled. "Give us Polycarp!"

Upon a magistrate's order, soldiers dashed out of the arena to find him.

When they heard the news, Polycarp's friends urged him to escape. So he moved to another farm. There he prayed that God's will would be done. Three days before his arrest, Polycarp, while at prayer, had a vision. In it he saw that the pillow under his head burst into flames and burned to a cinder. When he awoke, he interpreted the dream to those present, telling them, "No doubt Jesus wants me to share Christ's suffering. I'm going to depart from this life by fire."

Word came that his pursuers were near. The church members, loving him, urged him, "Move to another house, Polycarp." He complied, taking up residence on yet another farm.

There his pursuers gained ground in their search by arresting his servants and torturing them until they revealed Polycarp's location.

Late one night, these servants came to Polycarp's quarters before the authorities arrived and found him upstairs in bed. After apologizing for reporting his whereabouts to his pursuers, they pleaded with him to flee before it was too late. He could have moved to another residence and perhaps escaped capture, but he refused, saying, "God's will be done."

The soldiers arrived on the Sabbath.

When Polycarp heard that they'd arrived, he came down to meet them, greeting them in a cheerful, gentle manner. His pursuers, seeing him, marveled when they saw such a wonderful old man with a dignified, confident bearing. Among themselves they asked, "Why was there such an anxiety to arrest this man and bring him to justice?"

Meanwhile, Polycarp ordered that food be served to the soldiers there to arrest him. They sat at the table with him and were fed all that they could eat. In return, Polycarp asked, "May I be allowed to pray for one hour before joining you?" His wish was gladly granted.

While the soldiers continued eating, Polycarp stood and prayed, not for one hour, but for two. The soldiers were impressed with his prayer. He was so filled with God's grace that he even prayed for the soldiers—that they'd carry out their responsibilities well. As they listened, the soldiers became distressed that a man so godlike would be destroyed; nevertheless, when they couldn't eat another bite, and when Polycarp had finished praying, the soldiers had no choice but to fulfill their duty.

Polycarp willingly joined them.

Off they went. Riding donkey-back made for a slow journey. Eventually, they arrived at a main road, where the soldiers introduced Polycarp to the chief of police, whose name just happened to be Herod, and to Herod's father, named Nicetes.

After transferring Polycarp to a carriage, Herod and Nicetes sat beside him and tried persuasion. "What would be the harm in saying, 'Lord Caesar,' and burning a little incense as a sacrifice to him?" Herod asked. Nicetes added, "You'd be safe then."

At first Polycarp made no answer. When pressed, he replied, "I have no intention of taking your advice."

Persuasion having failed, Herod and his father abandoned their niceties and turned to threats. Stopping the carriage, they pushed Polycarp out so quickly that his leg was injured. But Polycarp walked on toward the stadium as if nothing had happened.

When it was announced that Polycarp had been arrested, the crowd roared, "Polycarp has been arrested!"

A loud chant ensued, "Polycarp! Polycarp! We want Polycarp!"

As he entered the arena, the noise of the crowd was deafening. But one voice was heard above the ruckus declaring, "Be strong, Polycarp, and play the man!" No one saw the speaker. It could have been the cry of a fellow Christian who was sitting in the stadium, or it could have come from heaven itself. One thing is certain, though, not a few who were in attendance reported hearing it.

Polycarp was taken before the proconsul, who said, "Respect your years!" Then he added, "Swear by Caesar's fortune, change your attitude, and say, 'Away with *the atheists*!' "

Polycarp knew that when the proconsul asked him to curse "the atheists," he meant all those who didn't worship *all* the gods of Rome; however, Polycarp thought of a different interpretation. With his face set, and I imagine a twinkle of mischief in his eyes and perhaps a smile on his face, he turned to the crowd in the stadium, waved his hand toward them, and proclaimed, "Away with the atheists!"

The proconsul then realized that to Polycarp an "atheist" was someone who did not know the Christian God. Unimpressed, he said, "Swear and I'll set you free. Curse Christ!"

Polycarp answered, "For eighty and six years I've served Him, and He's done me no wrong; why should I blaspheme my King, who's saved me?"

The proconsul replied, "Swear by Caesar's fortune!"

Polycarp retorted, "If you imagine me to swear by Caesar's fortune, as you put it, pretending not to know what I am, I'll tell you plainly: I *am* a Christian. If you wish to study Christian doctrine, choose a day and you'll hear it."

The proconsul shot back, "Convince the people!"

Polycarp replied, "I think it's proper for me to discuss these things with you. We have been taught to render to authorities the honor that is due them. But as to the people, I do not consider them the proper persons to whom to make my defense."

The proconsul replied, "I have wild beasts. I'll throw you to them if you don't change your attitude."

"Call them!" Polycarp replied. "Bring them on. We Christians cannot change our attitude if it means a change from the better to the worse, but it is a noble thing to change from wickedness to righteousness."

The governor stated, "If you make light of the beasts, I'll have you destroyed by fire, unless, of course, you decide to alter your attitude."

Polycarp answered, "The fire you threaten with burns for a while and is extinguished. There's a fire you know nothing about—the fire of judgment to come. That fire is reserved for the ungodly." The face of the proconsul turned pale momentarily at the thought that the gods might judge him unfavorably.

"But why do you hesitate? Do what you want!" In all that he spoke, Polycarp was filled with courage and joy. His features were full of grace. What he said didn't alarm the judges; rather, they were amazed. Then they set the crier to announce, "Polycarp has confessed to being a Christian." It was announced three times.

At this time the entire crowd of Smyrnaeans—Gentiles and Jews alike—yes, many Jews were there seated before the arena on the Sabbath when they should've been keeping the day holy, clamored to see a Christian destroyed. Some thought that the Jews shouted louder than the Gentiles, so eager were they to see the followers of Christ punished.

The crier went on to announce, "Polycarp is a teacher in Asia, the father of Christians, the destroyer of our gods, who teaches numbers of people not to sacrifice or even worship—"

When the crowd heard this, their deafening shouts drowned out the rest of the crier's announcement. They yelled passionately, "Deliver Polycarp to the lions!"

Soon they were chorusing, "Give Polycarp to the lions! To the lions! Bring out the lions! To the lions for Polycarp! To the lions! Lions! Lions! Feed Polycarp to the lions!"

Frowning, the governor raised his hand and waited until the shouts died down. Shaking his head from side to side, he objected, "It's illegal to let the lions out because the sport has been shut down for the day."

Initially the crowd booed and hissed; then someone shouted, "Burn

Polycarp alive!" Soon everyone was shouting, "Send Polycarp to the flames. Tie him to the stake. Burn him alive!"

"Burn Polycarp! Burn Polycarp! Burn Polycarp!" the crowd chanted.

Polycarp remembered his dream about the burning pillow and realized he'd interpreted it correctly. His dream was about to be fulfilled.

The crowds rushed out of the stadium to collect wood from workshops and public baths. The Jews, joining in with more enthusiasm than the rest because it involved a Christian, spent their own money for whatever was necessary for the pyre. (In buying the material, had the Jews forgotten it was the Sabbath?)

When the pyre was ready, Polycarp took off his outer garment, loosened his belt, and tried to remove his shoes, but it was something he was unaccustomed to doing. Usually the church members, who'd desired to honor him because of his virtuous life, had eagerly taken them off for him, even before his hair had grayed. There was no time for hesitation now as the instruments for the burning were assembled around him.

When guards came to tie him to the post and nail him in place, Polycarp cried, "Leave me as I am. He who enables me to endure the fire will enable me, even if you don't secure me with nails, to remain on the pyre without shrinking."

So they agreed to secure him without nails. He put his hands behind him and he was bound like a noble ram, or like Isaac by his father Abraham, about to be a sacrifice for the Lord Almighty.

Then Polycarp prayed, "O, God, thank You for letting me be a martyr today. Let me show these people that Christians aren't afraid of death. I claim Your promise of resurrection. I know that You can resurrect my soul as an immortal body that is imperishable. Now please accept this humble sacrifice—may it be sweet smelling fragrance to You. You're the God of truth who cannot lie. I praise You and Your Son, who is the High Priest, and the Holy Spirit. May all glory go to You both now and in the age to come. Amen."

When he completed his prayer, the guards lit the fire, and a great flame shot up. Then the crowd saw a marvelous sight. Many report that the fire took the shape of a vaulted room, something like the ship's sail in the wind that made a wall around the martyr's body. It did not resemble a burning fire, but silver or gold being refined in a furnace. Indeed, some reported that they smelled a wonderful fragrance, not like that of flesh, but more like a breath of frankincense or some other costly spice.

Seeing that the body didn't burn, the arena's *confector*\* was summoned to run his sword through Polycarp.

When he did so, those who witnessed the event recalled that so much blood gushed out that it extinguished the flame. Others seemed to remember seeing a dove flying overhead in the sky.

All who saw this marveled at the difference between what happens in the arena to Christians as opposed to what happened to other men. It was clear to them that Polycarp belonged to God's elect. Those who witnessed the martyrdom spread the news. It was talked about for a couple hundred years until the story was recorded by Eusebius, the father of church history. In fact, it's one of the better documented martyrdoms in early Christianity, preserved to this day as a final testimony of a godly man. Some who witnessed or heard of Polycarp's martyrdom became interested in Christianity and learned about Jesus Christ.

It was the witness of men like Polycarp who prompted the historian Tertullian to write, "The blood of the martyrs is seed."

---

\* A confector's duty in the arena was to put down injured animals.

# Disguised as a Muslim to Go to Church

The white walls were bare except for family pictures hanging near the ceiling and a stereo system next to the door where shoes lay piled outside. The family waited for their daughter, Mariam, to serve the food. She set out plates of rice, hummus, tabouli, and a spicy olive oil called *zeit,* then placed a flat bread called *sharkh* at the center of the table.

Mariam joined her family as they dipped the *sharkh* into the *zeit.* When they were nearly finished eating, she mustered the courage to make her announcement. She feared her father would be furious. "Daddy," Mariam blurted nervously, "I'm not going to church with you on Sunday."

"Why not?" Her father's voice sounded guarded.

"I'm going to a different church that studies the Bible."

"Where'd you get *that* silly idea?" her father shouted. "Mariam, you're going to church with *us*! Go to your room and think it over." Mariam obeyed.

In her room, she had plenty of time to think. For her, growing up Christian in an Islamic region where Nebuchadnezzar had once ruled was both easy and difficult. Babylon lay in ruins near her hometown of Baghdad, thus proving Bible prophecy, yet the Ba'ath Party government made it illegal for Christians to share their faith with their Muslim neighbors or to proclaim their beliefs outside of a church.

Mariam loved attending her family's church. She reveled in the ritual, appreciated the prayer, sincerely sang the songs, and believed in the Bible. She celebrated the ceremony from the depths of her heart. But the family's church didn't study the Bible enough.

From reading the Bible herself, she'd discovered passages differing from her church's teaching. Her priest's explanation hadn't satisfied her. Mariam wanted to follow the truth.

That was why her father banished her to her room. Mariam loved her parents dearly and wanted to please them. Should she obey them and go to their church, or should she do what she believed the Bible taught? That was her dilemma. She must persuade them to let her go to a church that taught Scripture. But how?

Her mother interrupted her thoughts. "Time to fix supper."

"Yes, Mother." Mariam went to the kitchen. When her father sat down to eat, she expected him to discuss church, but he didn't. She felt relieved, but when should she ask again to attend a church that studied the Bible?

She crossed off the days on her calendar but didn't dare ask. On Friday, she decided procrastination had to end. At supper, everyone seemed relaxed. The time seemed right. "Daddy?" Her voice squeaked, but no one else noticed, "May I go to church this weekend?"

"Of course," her father replied. "We'll go together."

"I'm not going with you."

"You are not going anywhere unless I say so!" Her father scowled menacingly.

"Please?" Mariam mustered her sweetest smile.

"We've discussed this already!" Her father exploded. "No school for you next week. Stay in your room unless you're cooking or eating until you've learned your lesson about obedience!"

Mariam went to her room. She wondered how she'd get to church now that she was grounded. She felt sorry for angering her father, but didn't know what else she could have done. As the hours ticked by, she devised a plan.

After breakfast the next morning, Mariam returned to her room and opened her closet. Someone had raided it. One of each pair of her shoes and socks was gone! She could never attend church in shoes and socks that didn't match.

To make matters worse, her church dress was missing. She knew she couldn't ask her parents what happened to her church clothes. She guessed her brother had entered her room while she was fixing breakfast. Momentarily, she conceded defeat. But then an idea popped in her mind.

She walked unnoticed through the kitchen, slipped outside, knocked on her Muslim neighbor's door, and asked to borrow some clothes from her. The neighbor brought out a *chador*—traditional Muslim attire, which is a full-length black robe and a black veil that covered everything except the wearer's eyes. The robe even covered her toes. Mariam had never worn such clothing, but thought it was perfect. Wearing it, she could walk the streets without revealing her identity.

Her neighbor helped her put it on. Once clad, Mariam thanked her neighbor and headed to her friend Marta's house. Mariam and Marta were about the same size. And Marta attended a church that taught from the Bible.

Marta didn't recognize Mariam until she spoke. "Marta, it's Mariam." When Mariam told Marta about her mismatched shoes and socks and missing dress, both girls laughed.

"That's why you are wearing a Muslim robe," Marta said between giggles.

"I want to go to church with you," Mariam said, turning serious, "but I haven't a thing to wear. Marta, do you have an extra dress I could borrow?"

"Which dress would you like?" The two girls searched Marta's closet until Mariam chose one. Soon she joined Marta and her family on their way to church. They carried Bibles so they could study the preacher's message.

After church, Mariam asked Marta if she could stay at her house for a few days. "I'm grounded from school, Marta. It's punishment for going to church today. I want to change schools. I want to attend a Christian school and get a Christian education. I don't have any money, but I'll work." Marta asked her parents, and they agreed that Miriam could live with them for a while.

Back in Mariam's house, lunchtime arrived and Mariam was missing. The family panicked, worried about their daughter. When someone told them she had gone to church, the panic became rage. They sent search parties to bring her home, but were unable to find her for several weeks.

Mariam's family missed her cheery ways. They missed her fixing food and setting the table. They longed to hear her voice again. She had run away because she had been forbidden to go to a church that studied the Bible. The family knew she loved them. *Were we too harsh?* they wondered. *Mariam isn't a bad girl. If she will return home,* they resolved, *we will let her worship at any church she likes.*

The neighbors learned that the family was looking for Mariam. One day the phone rang. Sami, a friend of the family, said, "Mariam and I attend the same Christian school. Your daughter is living with the principal's family and she's working."

"I'm glad to know she's safe," Mariam's father said. "Do you have her phone number?" Sami dictated the number. As soon as he hung up, Mariam's father dialed the principal's number. The principal answered.

"Hello. May I speak to Mariam?"

"She's at work."

"Oh, where's she working?"

"She's a janitor."

"A *what!*" her father exploded.

"She's doing a fine job cleaning the school."

"My daughter doing menial tasks—impossible!" he yelled into the receiver. "We're a high-class family. My daughter *cannot* be a *janitor!*"

"Mariam works to pay her school fees." The principal replied calmly. "It costs money to attend a Christian school."

The father thought for a moment. *Mariam wants to attend a Christian school, but she can't afford it. She ran away from home to attend a church that studies the Bible. I have been hard on her. If she doesn't have money, she can't attend school without earning her way. But she shouldn't disgrace the family by working as a janitor.* "It's final. She may not do dirty work. Tell her to quit."

"But what about paying for her tuition?" The principal asked.

"We're a wealthy family. Send her tuition bills to me. I'll pay them all."

That's how Mariam was able to continue her education at a Christian school and continue attending a church that studied the Bible.

# God's Time and a Tube of Toothpaste

**M**r. Yen, who was a Seventh-day Adventist Christian, lived in Tai-wan during the Japanese occupation. He'd been reading Tolstoy and other nineteenth-century Russian authors who were pacifists and opposed to war; then World War II began. Naturally, considering his reading material, he decided he wouldn't fight. When asked to serve his country, he refused to bear arms and requested permission to attend church every Saturday. Both requests were immediately denied.

Instead, Mr. Yen was sent to prison. When he arrived at the prison, he discovered that this wooden-walled prison was surrounded by barbed wire. The gate was a row of upright logs strapped tightly together. A couple of guards yanked one of the logs free and shoved Mr. Yen toward the gap. "Enter!" one of them ordered. Expecting them to pull out an-other log so he could more easily comply, Mr. Yen stood still. But when they pushed him again, he obeyed.

After squeezing sideways between the logs, Mr. Yen saw the guards slam the log back into place, trapping him inside. Looking around, he discovered that there were two sections inside. In the center of the log-walled prison was a courtyard surrounded by another coiled barbed-wire fence. A guard directed Mr. Yen to enter the door on the right.

Once inside, he found two rows of inmates leaning against the log wall. There was no place for him to sit except near the entrance. Mr. Yen learned that new prisoners always sat next to the door. They could move to a new location only when someone left and made room. The farther one sat along the wall indicated how long one had been incarcerated.

When Mr. Yen sat down, the others asked, "Why are you here?"

Boldly, he replied, "I'm a Christian who asked the army to let me go to church on Saturday. I requested not to carry a gun because I don't believe in war."

Some of the prisoners rolled their eyes and others hissed. "So what happened?" one asked.

"My requests are being considered. In the meantime, I wait here!"

"That was stupid," some of the prisoners jeered. Others said, "I'd rather comply than come here!"

Still others bragged about their crimes, saying, "Next time I'll do better and not get caught! Unfortunately, until I'm released, it's my sad fate to live in jail because my parents didn't raise me right."

As Mr. Yen listened to their stories, he detected a common thread running through them. Nothing was ever their fault—except when they had gotten caught. As the inmates began talking about other things, one or two of them mumbled, "Mr. Yen was courageous to stand up for what he believes." Hearing the prisoners' foul talk, Mr. Yen felt out of place and grew discouraged.

Because the cell lacked enough space for the inmates to sleep comfortably on their backs, they had to stretch out on their sides and were pressed tightly against the cell mates on either side of them. The room was narrow, forcing the prisoners to extend their legs across the center of the room and next to the prisoner against the opposite wall. Mr. Yen soon felt as if he were a sardine in a can.

Next to Mr. Yen stood a basket atop some barbed wire that functioned as the toilet. Initially he considered himself lucky to be lying beside it, because he didn't want to have to step on the carpet of humanity to relieve himself at night. He soon changed his mind and could hardly wait for another prisoner to arrive so he wouldn't need to sit by the entrance.

Sadly for Mr. Yen, no new prisoners arrived for a long time.

Finally, one day another prisoner arrived. Tired of repeating their own stories, the inmates wanted to hear a fresh story. Perhaps no one was more excited to have a new cell mate than Mr. Yen. At last he could move away from the basket!

Then it seemed that many more prisoners arrived. Soon Mr. Yen reached the middle of the wall. By this time, he frequently thought about the Chinese writing character for *prisoner*—it portrayed a person surrounded by four walls.

When he felt depressed, which was more often than not, he asked God, "Why am I here?" He looked at those around him and declared to God, "These people aren't my kind of people! Please, get me out!"

But when he felt good, he sang, "What a Friend We Have in Jesus."

The prisoner sitting next to him liked the song and asked Mr. Yen to teach it to him. So he tried. The two became good friends. Mr. Yen told him his address and said, "I'll be released soon. God will set me free!"

"Are you sure?" his friend asked.

"I'm certain!"

"What makes you certain? How do you know?"

"Because I'm not supposed to be here!" Mr. Yen asserted. "I'm supposed to be doing God's work, not wasting time in here."

"Shall we sing that song about your Friend Jesus again?" his friend asked. Then the two sang together. But Mr. Yen's friend wasn't very educated. Though he learned the words, he could sing the song only with the five-note scale used in typical Chinese music, so the hymn sounded more like a Chinese folk opera than church music. Singing in two-part harmony was out of the question. Hearing the man attempt to sing a hymn written for an eight-note scale on a five-note scale made Mr. Yen despondent.

He prayed, *What am I doing here with these scoundrels? Why did You put me here? It must be a mistake. I can't teach these guys anything—not even how to sing! I want out!* he demanded, thinking it would show God his great faith. *I'll make a deal with You, God,* he continued. *I'll stay here until my toothpaste is gone. Then get me out, OK?* Convinced that God would answer his prayer, Mr. Yen began using more than his usual amount of toothpaste. Instead of brushing once daily as had become his custom in jail, he brushed three times a day. He wanted to use up the toothpaste quickly so God would get him home sooner.

But when the toothpaste was gone, Mr. Yen wasn't released. The guard issued him another tube.

Again he said the same prayer, *God, when this tube is gone, I want out.* He kept to his new regimen of brushing his teeth three times daily, but when the tube was empty, he still wasn't released.

In the meantime, he tried to teach his friend other hymns, but the results grated on his ears, causing him to quit trying.

Throwing up his hands in despair, he prayed, *Lord, have You heard this man sing?* He paused as if awaiting an answer. *Doesn't his music hurt Your ears? It hurts mine! If I don't get out soon, I'll go mad like some of the other prisoners who've been here for a long time.*

Then an idea struck him.

Mr. Yen decided to make his deal with God public. Holding up his tube of toothpaste, he shouted so that everyone in the cell could hear, "God, when this tube is finished, get me out!" Most of the prisoners ignored him, but a few listened. Some scoffed, and one or two said, "We'll see about that," but Mr. Yen didn't care. Sitting back comfortably, he smiled to himself, thinking that this time God would have to honor his request because His honor was at stake. Surely God would want to save face.

God didn't do what Mr. Yen thought he could force Him to do.

Mr. Yen went through many tubes of toothpaste.

A year later, however, he was released and allowed to return home. By that time he knew how it felt to be in deep depression. He wanted to forget about that miserable prison. If he never saw those horrible inmates again, he'd have been pleased. He just wanted to put the whole experience behind him.

But God had other plans.

A few months after his release, Mr. Yen answered a knock at his door. Standing before him was his former cell mate—the one who couldn't sing hymns. "I've been released," he announced. "I have nowhere to go. Then I remembered that you called me 'friend' and even gave me your address."

Mr. Yen knew that was true.

Then his friend said, "May I stay at your house for a while?"

Without hesitation, Mr. Yen agreed. Soon they were reminiscing about the old hymn "What a Friend We Have in Jesus."

The former inmate told Mr. Yen, "I was impressed with you in prison. You were different from the rest. I want to know Jesus as my Friend." So they studied together. When the former prisoner learned about Jesus' love and teachings, he was excited. He longed to tell others about his new Friend named Jesus.

He began selling books about Jesus to anyone who would buy them. Recently, Mr. Yen, who was living in Hong Kong when he told this story, returned to Taiwan and visited this former cell mate. He has a family and lives in a lovely house. He's become the top Christian book salesman on the island.

When Mr. Yen looks back at his prison experience, he thinks about his bargain with God—and his oft-repeated question, "Why am I here—and why don't You get me out now?" He now knows that God has His own purposes and His own time. God sent him to prison to meet a prisoner. God's plan had been for him to reach that prisoner because He knew that that man would become a servant for Jesus.

Whenever Mr. Yen thinks God is moving too slowly, he looks at a tube of toothpaste. *God is in control,* he reminds himself. *He'll take care of everything in His own good time.* Then he chuckles as he reminds himself, *Someday I'll understand the reason for His delay when the answer comes knocking on my door!*

# The Bushman and the Shining One

Here's an old story that Spencer Maxwell, my great-uncle, used to tell. He worked in East Africa for forty years. Maxwell Adventist Academy in Nairobi, Kenya, was so named to honor him. The nomadic Bushmen tribes live in Africa's Kalahari Desert. They move from place to place, hunting for food and shelter. Skilled in desert survival, they are superb trackers who can "read" the land. They often use ostrich eggs as canteens and sometimes fill the eggs with water, seal the holes with beeswax, and bury the eggs for later use.

A unique trait about Bushmen is their eating habits. It's not often that a tribe can catch a good meal, so when the men kill some large game, such as an antelope, the tribe eats the entire animal in one sitting. The Bushmen's bellies grow rather large, so large that they make both the men and the women look pregnant. After eating all the available food, the tribe hibernates until all the food is digested. Sometimes it takes days. Then they wake up and hunt for food again.

The Bushmen's language is unusual too. It's explosive, with many pops and clicks of the tongue. In the written language, the tongue clicks are indicated by an *X* followed by an exclamation mark.

Sometime in the early 1950s, a member of one of these Bushmen tribes had an unusual dream. In the morning, he still remembered it. When he was alone with his family, he said, "Last night I had a dream." They were interested, so he continued. "I saw a bright light. As my eyes adjusted, I noticed the light was in the form of some being. The Shining One told me many curious things. Most of the time, he talked about a people of the Book and said that I was to learn from them. Oh, I almost forgot. He taught me to talk real funny. Listen!" He went around pointing to objects and calling them funny names. His family laughed to hear such strange sounds. "The Shining One said these funny words will help me communicate with the people of the Book. To find these funny-talking people, the Shining One told me to walk east." It all seemed so mysterious yet so important. He couldn't stop thinking about the dream. Eventually, he shared it with the other members of his tribe. They decided that he should find these people of the Book.

So he set out. He walked and walked for about 150 miles until he came to a village. These villagers were not Bushmen, but Bantus. They were a taller race and couldn't speak his language. Traditionally, Bantus and Bushmen were enemies, but the little Bushman reminded himself that the Shining One had sent him to find a Bantu to learn about the Book. Suddenly, he remembered, "I better talk funny now."

A villager saw the little Bushman and hailed him, saying, "I see you." (That is the way a Bantu says Hello.)

"I see you," the little Bushman answered in kind.

The villager was amazed. "How is it you can speak my language?"

The little Bushman told the Bantu about his dream. "The Shining One taught me your language," he explained. Then he asked, "Are you one of the people of the Book?"

The Bantu was a Christian. He immediately knew what the little Bushman meant. "Yes, we are," he said. "Let me take you to our pastor." So he led him to the pastor's home, and there the little Bushman repeated his story about the Shining One who had sent him on such a long journey. When he had finished, he asked, "Are you the people of the Book?"

The pastor smiled, went to his bookshelf, and pulled down a black book. As soon as the little Bushman saw it, he said, "That's it!" It was the Holy Bible. "That's the very Book I saw in my dream. You must be the people of the Book! May I learn from you?"

Naturally, the pastor was happy. He arranged for the Bushman to sleep in his house that night, saying, "We'll begin studies first thing in the morning."

At first, the little Bushman couldn't get to sleep. He was more accustomed to sleeping under a bush than on a soft bed. That night, while he slept, the Shining One appeared to him again in a dream. He told him, "The pastor is not one of the people of the Book because he doesn't worship on the seventh day. Look for a pastor named Moyo."

It was all rather strange to the little Bushman. He really didn't know what to do. He only knew that his journey wasn't over. Where was he to find Pastor Moyo?

The next morning, the little Bushman thanked the pastor for his hospitality. Then, speaking quite politely, he said, "I had another dream. The Shining One told me you are not one of the people of the Book because you don't keep the seventh day holy."

The pastor grew angry and said, "I showed you the Bible, and you said, 'That's it!' Because that's the Book you dreamed about, I must be a man of the Book. Now let's study as planned!"

The little Bushman politely insisted that the pastor was not a person of the Book. "The Shining One told me that the people of the Book worship on the seventh day of the week. Do you know a man named Moyo?"

The pastor refused to help. All he would say was, "Our village chief believes the same as I do. How can the chief be wrong? Let's go talk with him. Maybe he can help you understand your dream." So the pastor took the little Bushman to the chief.

The chief said, "I have translators, but, from what I hear, you don't need one. I want to hear you speak in my language."

The little Bushman smiled politely and related his story about his dream, his encounter with the Shining One, his 150-mile trek to find the people of the Book, and his meeting with the pastor in the chief's village. "I was so happy to discover the Book is the Holy Bible and that your pastor owns one." Then he told about his second dream, and asked, "Do you know anyone who worships on the seventh day?"

Actually, the chief's wife worshiped on the seventh day, but he was embarrassed to say so. He detested her religion.

The pastor hadn't said anything either because he feared that all his church members would leave his church if he directed the little Bushman to her. With no members, he'd have no church to lead! Not wanting to lose his position, he lied.

To no avail the little Bushman questioned the chief about a people who worshiped on the seventh day. Then he asked, "Do you know where Pastor Moyo is?"

The chief noticed that a large crowd of village folk was gathering. They disliked Bushmen because they were known to be dangerous. When offended, Bushmen kill the offender. Some had been hurt by Bushmen. Others had relatives who had. Some wanted revenge. Others were amazed to see a Bushman politely conversing with their chief in their own language.

Old resentments surfaced when they perceived that the Bushman was disagreeing with their chief. As anger spread through the crowd, the chief feared it could turn into a violent mob.

Having decided not to tell the truth about his wife, he was uncertain what to do next. As the villagers grew more restless, he feared for the little Bushman's safety. Soon, if he didn't do something, they would turn into a mob. Not wanting to be responsible for what might happen to the Bushman, the chief made a decision. He reasoned that if the little Bushman were found to have done nothing illegal, perhaps the crowd would calm down.

So he sent the Bushman to the white man. In South Africa, white people were seen by the indigenous people as just another tribe. Usually, they dealt with legal matters. In his village, a white South African of British ancestry handled legal matters.

He told the crowd to follow the little Bushman to the white man's home. "He'll determine whether the Bushman has broken the law." Seeing that the crowd was temporarily satisfied, the chief felt pleased with himself. He'd gotten rid of the Bushman without bloodshed. *Let the white man pacify the crowd,* he thought to himself.

The disgruntled crowd entered the white man's courtroom. Escorted by the pastor, the Bushman came to the front and began to relate his story.

The Englishman was deeply impressed. Before him stood a Bushman who claimed that a Shining One had taught him in a dream how to speak with the Bantus in their own language. He had to admit that the Bushman could speak it perfectly. This gave credence to the rest of the story. Just to make sure, he questioned the Bushman, but was unable to trip him up. He stuck to his story. Then the Bushman asked his advice. The white man thought about the legality of the story and found that no law had been broken. Hitting the podium with his gavel, he ordered the crowd to leave.

Reluctantly, the villagers obeyed. Soon only the pastor and the Bushman remained. The Englishman told the pastor he was free to go.

"Do you know where I can find the people of the Book?" the Bushman asked. The Englishman was at a loss for words.

That night, since no one would befriend him, the little Bushman did what most Bushmen do—he slept in the bush. Before he lay down, he prayed, "Shining One, please lead me to the real people of the Book. It seems no one else will."

In his sleep, he had another dream. The Shining One said, "You'll know Pastor Moyo because he owns a set of four volumes that are really nine."

The next morning, when he awoke, he saw a cloud. In most places, if you see a cloud, you think nothing of it. But in certain drier parts of Africa, clouds are special because they are so rare. When the little Bushman approached it, it moved. As he followed it, he realized it was the answer to his prayer. The Shining One was guiding him to Pastor Moyo! He followed the cloud for another 120 miles until he reached a town near a railway station located on the border of Rhodesia, now Zimbabwe. After the cloud had led him into the town, it vanished.

The Bushman rejoiced, knowing he was near the real people of the Book. Walking through the town, he asked everyone he met if they knew Pastor Moyo.

Eventually, someone led him to a pastor's home. When the little Bushman knocked on the door, a man opened it. "Are you Pastor Moyo?" the Bushman asked.

"I am." The pastor smiled. "How do you know my name?"

"It's a long story." The Bushman retold it. "Can you show me the Book?"

Pastor Moyo reached for his Bible.

"That's it!" the Bushman confirmed. "Do you worship on the seventh day?"

"I do," the pastor replied.

The little Bushman beamed. "One last question," he said excitedly. "Can you show me the four volumes that are really nine?"

Pastor Moyo went to his bookshelf and took down a set of Ellen G. White's *Testimonies for the Church*. In that particular edition, the nine volumes were bound into four books.

Unable to contain himself, the Bushman exclaimed, "Those are the very books I saw in my dream! My journey is finally at an end! At last I've found the real people of the Book." He asked Pastor Moyo to teach him. They studied the Bible and Ellen White's writings.

The Bushman believed what he was taught. He asked Pastor Moyo to visit his people and teach them. The Bushman became the first of his people to be baptized as a Seventh-day Adventist. Soon there was a Bushman church of about twenty members.

Because their lives are hard, Bushmen don't live long. A few years after his 270-mile quest to find the people of the Book, the little Bushman died—at the ripe old age of fiftysomething.

If it hadn't been for the little Bushman's dream about the Shining One and his trek to find Pastor Moyo, it might have taken much longer before any Bushmen accepted Seventh-day Adventist Christianity. This story has been told and retold time and again, for it is truly a remarkable testimony of God's guidance in human history.

# The Nazi Who Came to Church

**B**ubby hated going to church. He wanted to be a soccer player, but to join the school team, he was required to practice on Friday nights and play on Saturdays. Because he truly was a good player, his friends asked him to play, but he couldn't. When they asked why, he was too ashamed to say.

He was ashamed of being a Seventh-day Adventist because the denomination had no church building in Rotterdam, Netherlands, so the church members met in the basement of a bicycle-repair shop. The one good thing about the location was that if his friends saw him enter the shop, they wouldn't guess he was attending a worship service. If they knew, they might ask why he worshiped on the seventh day, which, he thought, would be too much to explain.

Every Sabbath morning Bubby did his best to avoid being seen on his way to church. If he spotted his school friends, he ran as fast as he could into the church because he didn't want anyone to see him go inside.

His mother thought otherwise. She always told everyone that her son loved to attend church. "He can't get there fast enough," she'd say. Then she would add affectionately, "He loves church so much that he runs most of the way there."

One day all that changed. World War II was raging, and in Rotterdam, the Dutch marines were fighting the Nazis paratroopers. Soldiers with machine guns were firing in the streets outside their home.

On Sabbath morning, Bubby's father looked out the window and saw the empty street. Turning to his wife, he said, "There's not even a dog on the streets! We can't go to church today. Maybe we'd better stay home."

Not wanting to go to church anyway, Bubby agreed with his father. But his mother said, "We're going to church."

So they donned their Sabbath best and went.

On the streets, they met a soldier who held up his hand and ordered, "Stop! Go home. It's too dangerous to be outside."

Mother explained, "We're going to church."

The soldier wrinkled his nose. Then his eyes brightened. "You must be mixed up, ma'am. The war is confusing everyone. Tomorrow is church day, not today. Go home!"

Mother said, "No, today *is* the day we go to church." She whipped out her Bible and showed him Exodus 20. " 'Six days shalt thou labour, and do all thy work: But the seventh day is the Sabbath of the Lord thy God,' " she read (Exodus 20:9, 10, KJV).

That was too much for him. "I need orders," he announced and disappeared. He returned with his sergeant. His orders to the waiting family were the same: "Go home! It's too dangerous!"

"We want to go to church," Mother explained.

He said, "No. Go tomorrow, not today."

"No," Mother insisted. "We're going to church today, not tomorrow." She added, "Tomorrow's the wrong day."

Puzzled, the sergeant wrinkled his forehead. Suddenly, a broad smile spread across his face. "Did you say you were going to 'church' today?" he asked. "Don't you mean 'synagogue'?"

"We're not Jewish!" Mother exclaimed emphatically. With Nazis around, Mother didn't want to be considered Jewish. "We're Christians."

"Christians?" he asked. "And you go to church *today*?" His eyes clouded in confusion. Out came Mother's Bible and she turned the pages to

Exodus 20 and Deuteronomy 5. "You see, God said to remember the seventh day." She showed them what Jesus said about keeping the Sabbath. She continued, "The disciples worshiped on the seventh day after Jesus' resurrection and ascension."

Mother's information overpowered the sergeant. Turning, he said, "I need orders. I'll be back. Don't go anywhere." With that he left and returned with a lieutenant, who predictably held up his hand and asserted, "It's too dangerous today—go home!"

Mother patiently explained that they were going to church.

"What denomination are you?" the lieutenant asked.

"Seventh-day Adventist," Mother replied.

He smiled. "I understand. Go ahead." After shaking hands with them, he again warned them of the dangers, adding, "I hope God will go with you—you'll need His help to make it to church alive."

The family faced many harrowing experiences on the way to church that day. Bubby thought they'd find the church empty. Dreading the return trip, he thought surely they were foolish and wasting time.

Eventually, they arrived at the old bicycle repair shop. When they reached the basement, Bubby didn't want to open the door. But when they stepped inside, it was obvious that every church member was present. A deacon ushered the family to their usual seats in the front row.

Walking down the aisle of the packed church, Bubby felt proud to be part of a group that were willing to risk their lives to be together with God. He asked himself, *Is it possible that a church is not merely made of brick and stone, but of hearts and minds? Perhaps,* he thought, *the building isn't as important as the fellowship inside.*

A commotion at the door interrupted his thoughts. A Nazi soldier stood in the doorway.

"Nazi!" the elder yelled at him. "Go away! Isn't it enough that you're destroying our city? Why do you have to come here?"

Everyone waited apprehensively for the soldier's response.

"I'm a believer," the German said. "I've come to worship! May I come in?"

The church fell silent as all eyes turned to the elder. The church members well knew that the elder had once owned a business that had made him considerably wealthy and that the Nazis had not only destroyed his business but his home as well. He had gone quite literally from riches to poverty overnight. While times were tough for everyone, they were especially so for him. All in the room resented the Nazis for occupying their homeland, but they knew that the head elder had every reason to despise a soldier representing the Third Reich. Anxiously they waited, wanting to know what the elder would do.

The elder hesitated and swallowed hard; then he hurried across the room and threw his arms around the German. "If you're a believer, you're one of us. You're welcome here!" He escorted the soldier down the aisle to a front-row seat.

Realizing for the first time that his Seventh-day Adventist church loved everyone, friend and foe, Bubby felt doubly proud to be part of such a group. From that day on, Bubby loved going to church. He soon discovered that he had a large family of uncles and aunts. Yet, oddly enough, none of his newfound uncles and aunties were even distantly related to him. Bubby's mother was Lithuanian and his father's family was from a different part of the Netherlands. He was considered family simply because he was a Seventh-day Adventist.

Once fearful that his friends wouldn't like him if they knew he was a Seventh-day Adventist, he now proudly introduced them to his new family. Whenever he visited the home of some church members, they always shared some milk, which, due to the war rationing, was scarce. If he had a classmate with him, they were more than happy to share with his classmates too. They knew that if the shoe were on the other foot, Bubby would share his rationed milk with them. Everyone took care of everyone else.

For Bubby, everything changed for him that Sabbath when the Nazi soldier showed up at church. On that day he learned that a church is not just a building, but the people who worship there.

# Sabbath Prayer

## Part 1: Acting Debut

**S**ometimes God works through faulty humans even when they make mistakes. Here is a story about a mistake Justin made, but God worked it out for good.

Most people go to Hong Kong to do shopping. That wasn't why Justin went there. He went to this formerly British enclave off the coast of southern China to break into journalism and acting. Did I mention anything about a girl? Yes, there's a girl in the story. So, another reason why Justin moved to Hong Kong was because he'd met a girl who worked there, who'd claimed, "You can easily find a job in Hong Kong." He believed her. She also had said, "When you find one, call me. Here's my number." How could he lose?

Because he knew it would take some time to start writing articles and

acting, Justin made his day job teaching English in Macau, then a Portu-
guese colony located about forty-five minutes by boat from Hong Kong.
On the weekends, he slept in the dormitory at Chongking Mansions in
Kowloon, Hong Kong.

The dormitories in Chongking Mansions were not fancy. All a tenant
got was a bunk bed, a locker, and access to a kitchen. But people wanted
to sleep in Chongking Mansions because they knew what anyone who
wasn't a tourist knew—that, while they slept, casting directors from
Hong Kong's movie and television studios would look at everyone sleeping in the bunks and consider the possibility of placing one of them in
front of one of their cameras. Justin knew that if they liked what they
saw, he could get his start on the silver screen. Not a few famous actors
came from Hong Kong television and movie studios, including Jet Li,
John Lone, and Jackie Chan. Of course, it was only television extras who
were selected in Chongking Mansions, not those famous guys. Even as
an extra, though, it was anybody's guess as to who one might get to work
with if put on the set.

Night after night, he waited. At least he was asleep, so the waiting
didn't seem so long. Nevertheless, Justin began to wonder if these casting
directors were something like the tooth fairy.

Then it happened. It actually happened. All his nights sleeping in the
dormitory paid off. A casting director, as he walked among the sleeping
forms in the dormitory, looked at Justin's 130-pound, six-foot-tall frame,
together with his auburn hair, and imagined him as a British soldier.

That morning Justin was awakened by a tap on his shoulder. When he
opened his eyes, there was a strange face smiling at him. "Hi," the man
said, "I'm a casting director, and you look like a British soldier to me."
He extended his hand and Justin shook it.

"It's an honor to meet you," Justin said. Clad in a red-and-green-
striped polo shirt with faded blue jeans and a Panasonic baseball cap, he
didn't exactly look like any casting director Justin had ever imagined, but
when he noticed the man's clipboard full of contracts, Justin was convinced.

"Your role will be a speakie with only one line in Cantonese." The
casting director began speaking in a rapid staccato. "You'll holler, 'Stop!'
to prevent harm from being done to a woman." When Justin later learned

that another sleeper in the dormitory had been selected to play a British soldier who *would* do harm to a beautiful woman, Justin was grateful that his sleeping form appeared innocent and upstanding.

"Don't worry about your line being in Cantonese," the casting director continued, "we'll tell you what to say as well as how and when to say it. Are you interested?"

Feeling as if he were still dreaming, Justin nodded.

"Sign here." The casting director pulled out a contract from his clipboard and clipped it on top of the stack. After pulling a pen from behind his ear, he hurriedly held it out to Justin and smiled expectantly.

Perhaps Justin momentarily hesitated because the casting director added, "We'll drive you there and back and be responsible for everything except your meals. You'll get one hundred fifty dollars. You can get your meals at the studio canteen for twenty to forty dollars if you're frugal— especially if you like Chinese food." He took a deep breath, perhaps for Justin's benefit. "If you're interested, sign here." He marked an *X* in front of a line at the bottom of the page.

Taking the pen eagerly, Justin signed. "Just let me get my stuff and check out before I join you." The receptionist, who was grinning knowingly when Justin came to the counter, congratulated him on his new job. "Maybe I see you on TV someday!" he said. Justin joined the casting director, and they took the rickety elevator down to the casting director's van.

Soon the van arrived at the studios. Justin was welcomed, escorted to the set, and told, "Wait here. Someone will come. Tell you what to do."

Someone brought Justin his costume and helped him dress. Makeup artists painted his face. A stagehand took him to the spot where the action would take place, and he stood with other extras while the camera crew checked the lighting. A floppy sword was handed to him. "Use this," Justin was told.

"This can't hurt anyone," he laughed.

"Yeah." The stagehand smiled. "It looks pretty flimsy on set, but not on camera. Besides, it's against the law to use real weapons in the studio."

When the cameras aren't rolling on the set, actors, especially extras, have downtime, so Justin discovered he had a lot of time on his hands. Did I mention there was a girl in this story? Justin decided to call her.

"Hello, Jena," Justin said when she picked up the phone. "What's new?"

"I asked around and found a bilingual church we could attend," she answered.

"Tomorrow?" Attending church was a new idea for them; however, as they were getting to know each other better, Justin had suggested they might try attending church. He'd been raised a Seventh-day Adventist but was no longer going to services. "What day is tomorrow?"

"Sunday," Jena replied sweetly.

"Wrong day," Justin blurted out.

"I don't understand," she said. "You want to go to church, and I make an arrangement, but you don't want to go to a church because it's not the right day."

"Sunday is not the correct day of worship," Justin started to explain.

"Doesn't everybody worship on Sunday?" she asked,

"The Bible teaches that the seventh day is the Sabbath. It's a day of rest from work and a time to be with God."

"So why does everyone keep Sunday?" Jena asked.

"The Catholic Church takes credit for changing the day, and most Protestants follow the Catholic teaching."

"If tomorrow is the wrong day of worship, what are you doing today?" Jena asked.

Oops! Ever have one of those days when you woke up thinking it was a different day? That's what happened to Justin. Until this phone conversation, he'd thought it was Friday.

Sheepishly, he told Jena that he was working on a movie set as a British soldier. "It's my job to stop some bad people from hurting some British woman in the story."

"You just told me you aren't supposed to work on the Lord's Day. And that Saturday is the day to worship. What are you doing at a television studio?" It was a good question.

"Ah," Justin thought for a moment then decided to confess no matter how dumb it sounded. "I really forgot what day it is." Thinking it sounded bad, he added, "Let's just say that this is the first and last time I work on the Sabbath. It may mean that I'll never be able to work in a television studio again. Let's talk more about it over dinner."

Jena agreed. "I know a nice place overlooking the harbor." They hung up shortly after that.

Soon Justin was back on the set, standing head and shoulders taller than the other soldiers and looking brave as he commanded, "Stop!" in Cantonese and rescued the damsel in distress. But Justin couldn't enjoy it as much as before. He could hardly wait to leave.

The shot was in the can before sundown, and Justin was dropped off at the Chongking Mansions. He met Jena at an outdoor café. As they ate, Justin talked to her about the Sabbath as God intended it and how to keep it holy—to not do any work or enjoy one's own pleasure. It was a time to be with God.

"Can we attend church in the morning and work in the afternoon?" she asked before she stuffed a bite in her mouth.

"Many who keep Sunday take only the morning off from work, but the commandment says to keep the entire seventh day holy," Justin explained.

"That's all very well and good, but no one in Hong Kong can take a day off from work on Saturday." Jena's tone was harsh.

Justin looked over at the Hong Kong harbor. "Do you see that tower overhead?" he asked. "The one with the crocodile lighted in red."

"It's the main office for the Crocodile Shirt Company," Jena said.

"That's right."

"Last Christmas I bought you a wool V-neck sweater from one of their shops," Jena said.

"The manager of the Crocodile Shirt Company doesn't work on Sabbath," Justin said. Jena lifted her eyebrows and cocked her head sideways with interest. "He's the wealthiest Seventh-day Adventist alive today," Justin added. "All of his stores close from Friday night sundown and don't reopen until Saturday night after sundown."

Jena nodded, "You're right; they do."

"You noticed that?"

"Of course! They've been doing it since my childhood." A smile spread across her face.

"Did you know why they closed on Saturday?"

Jena looked down as she shook her head and frowned. Sipping orange juice from her straw, she looked straight into Justin's eyes and asked,

"Are they keeping what-do-you-call-it, um, that day you said is the right day to go to church?"

"Sabbath?" Justin answered with a smile. "Yes."

Jena was silent for a time. Her eyes drifted toward the crocodile-shaped red light shining atop the Crocodile Shirt Company tower. Then, almost to herself, she said, "If the Crocodile Shirt Company can keep Sabbath and succeed, I can, too. But I'll need to open up my own business."

"Don't make excuses for yourself," Justin urged. "Can't you negotiate with your boss to have a day off, or to work on Sunday instead?"

"I'm sorry, Justin. You don't know Chinese bosses!" Jena exclaimed. "They're the worst! That's why everyone in Hong Kong wants to be their own boss. If I asked for Sabbath off, I'd lose my job. The boss would just hire someone who *would* work whenever the boss wants. No," she concluded with a tone of finality, "the only way I can have Sabbaths off is to be my own boss, like the manager of the Crocodile Shirt Company."

"God will honor your faith," Justin said.

Jena looked at her watch. "We'd better go, or I'll miss the last bus."

"My bus is worse than yours, Jena. It will be a long walk home if I don't catch it." Hurriedly, they pushed back their chairs, dumped their dirty dishes in the trash, and headed for the nearest Mass Transit Railway (MTR) subway station that would carry them to their respective buses and homes.

Though still struggling with his own faith commitment, Justin knew he'd planted a seed in Jena's mind. *Will it take root and sprout?* That night Justin prayed that she'd agree to study the Bible with someone other than himself (as he feared she might feel unfair pressure if she took Bible studies from him) and learn more about God.

## Part 2: The Beauty Center

Jena was working on a facial massage for a client in the beauty center when the phone rang. She didn't answer, secretly hoping that it was for somebody else. She was on a tight schedule and didn't like to stop to talk with anyone. Fortunately, Eva, one of her colleagues, picked up the phone. The colleague said a few words, lay the receiver on the desk, and headed

toward Jena's room. Jena's heart sank. "Telephone," was all that Eva said.

Apologizing to the client, Jena told her she'd return quickly, hurried to the head office, and spoke into the receiver. It was Justin. "I'm busy with a client," Jena told him. "Can you make it quick?"

"You're where?" Jena asked. Justin always gave her the English names for places in Hong Kong, and Jena was used to their Chinese names. "Did you mean the Tsuen Wan Gong On Yuen?" she asked. That's the Tsuen Wan Adventist Hospital in English. He said it sounded about right. *Of course it does—I'm Chinese, so I speak the language!* Jena thought. *He thinks that since I live in a British territory, I should speak English—and he has a point.*

"What are you doing in the hospital?" Jena asked. "Please make it quick. I'm in a hurry.

"You're in a hospital bed? Why?" Jena looked at her watch. Time was passing. "I don't have time to talk," she said hastily. "I'll come to the hospital as soon as I get off work, OK? You can tell me everything. I've got to go—now—bye-bye." She hung up as soon as Justin bade her farewell and hurried back to her client.

Time fairly flew. Soon Jena was on the MTR subway heading to the hospital to see Justin. A few weeks before, Justin had told her he was going to Newbold College in England to meet his father, who was teaching a seminar. *Did something happen to Justin while he was overseas?* She worried, *Was he in an accident?*

Soon Jena was standing at the reception desk, asking which room Justin was in. When she peeked inside his room, she noticed that his body was covered in spots.

"What happened to you?" she asked.

"I've got chicken pox—"

"Chicken pox?" Jena interrupted. "Isn't that a childhood disease?"

"Yes, and it gets worse—"

"Worse," she interrupted again. "How?"

"It's worse for adults. In children, the spots are localized. In adults, they come wherever they want. I also have impetigo," Justin answered. He reached to rub the spots, then stopped. "It's itchy, but the doctor told me not to touch."

"You better take care of yourself," Jena said.

"Knock, knock!" A voice outside the curtain surrounding the bed said. A tall, thin American pushed the curtain aside. "I'm Chaplain Ron," he introduced himself. "I'm the one who met Justin at the airport and drove him here on his doctor's orders."

"Ah, Chaplain Ron," Justin said. "This is Jena—the young woman I met when I went hiking at Yellow Mountain in China. Afterward, she helped me find a bus when everyone else wanted me to take a taxi."

A broad smile spread across Chaplain Ron's face, "Well, hello, Jena!" He switched to Mandarin for a few minutes. Turning to Justin, he explained, "She says she went to a Catholic school in Hong Kong and knows a little bit about what Christians teach."

Chaplain Ron sat beside Justin's bed. "I wanted to check on you, Justin, as I'm the one with the best English in the hospital," he laughed. "Your doctor said he regretted letting you get on that plane to Hong Kong. While you were in midflight, he checked his medical books and discovered that the combination of chicken pox, impetigo, and high altitude could be fatal for you!"

"I arrived safely," Justin smiled impishly.

"Thank God you had an uneventful flight," Chaplain Ron replied. "All the same, your doctor wants to make sure the impetigo doesn't spread. He wanted the situation monitored here."

A nurse stepped in, carrying a small tray.

"These must be the creams the doctor ordered," Chaplain Ron surmised. He spoke with the nurse in Mandarin. "I was right," he said as he turned. "Well, it looks like you're in good hands. I'd best be moving on." As he exited, he called over his shoulder, "I'll be back!"

After the nurse left, Jena pulled out her cell phone, called the office, and requested time off from work. When she hung up, she told Justin she'd stay a day or two because it appeared the nurses were busy. Justin was concerned about how she'd sleep without a bed. She assured him she could sleep in the chair. "But you need me to make sure you get out of the hospital fast. I can rub the lotion on your back where it's hard for you to reach." Justin was happy with her offer.

When Chaplain Ron returned, Justin told him, "Jena will be staying in the hospital a couple of days."

"Well, isn't that grand," Chaplain Ron replied. "She'll take good care of you!"

Then Justin surprised Jena by asking Chaplain Ron a question. "Chaplain, as she might get bored here, would you be willing to give Bible studies to Jena?"

"That will depend on the young lady," Chaplain Ron replied, looking questioningly at Jena.

"I'd do it myself," Justin said. "But I'm afraid it would be a conflict of interest since we're both single."

"I understand," Chaplain Ron said. Turning to Jena, he asked, "Is that all right with you? Are you interested?"

Jena said she was.

"Good. The next time I come around, we can get started," Chaplain Ron said as he waved and excused himself.

And that's exactly what happened. Jena continued studying long after Justin was discharged with a clean bill of health. She was learning many things about an invisible God. She was born into a Buddhist home and had attended Catholic schools. The Catholics taught her to appreciate the Bible, but whether she worshiped at the cathedral or at a shrine, she always prayed to something visible. This invisible God was something new to her.

Sometimes she remembered her conversation with Justin when he told her about the Sabbath. The thought of a correct day to worship was in her mind, as was the example of the owner of the Crocodile Shirt Company, but she really didn't think much about it. Jena worked on the days she was scheduled because that's what employees are expected to do in Hong Kong.

She began working overtime so she could earn enough money to start her own business. One of her objectives in opening her own shop was to worship on the right day. Jena had a good location in mind, but the available real estate was pricey. The more time she spent looking, the more Jena felt something was not right.

She began to wonder, *Am I worshiping the true God? Is He real? Is He imaginary?*

She decided to talk with Eva, her colleague. When she told her about worshiping on the Sabbath, Eva said, "I've never heard about worshiping God on a right day. What is the Sabbath?"

"Remember the friend that we met in China on Yellow Mountain?" Jena asked.

"You mean Justin?" Eva replied.

"He told me that the seventh-day Sabbath is the correct day of worship." Jena explained, "He said we shouldn't work on that day."

"I think your friend is just lazy," Eva snorted. "He won't work on Saturday or Sunday. Christians, if they go to church at all, go on Sunday, not Saturday. My sister is Christian—she's working even on Sunday."

"I studied the Bible with a hospital chaplain," Jena continued. "He explained to me why they changed the day to Sunday from Saturday."

"How's that?" Eva asked.

"The Catholic Church changed it," Jena replied. "It isn't biblical."

"You're talking about all kinds of stuff I don't understand," Eva blurted.

"Eva," Jena looked her in the eye, "I want to follow what I've learned from the Bible about the Sabbath. I don't believe I can do that unless I have my own beauty center."

Eva's eyes brightened, "Ah, is that why you asked me to be your partner?"

Jena nodded. "Partially," she added. "The other reason is that I haven't got enough money to do it alone. I need your help."

"I see," Eva pursed her lips in thought. "You'll lose a lot of business," she cautioned. "Saturday is the busiest day in our line of work."

"I know," Jena nodded again. "I'll work on Sundays to make up for it," she added.

"I'll work on Saturday," Eva said. "I don't believe in the Bible."

"Eva, I don't know what to do," Jena ventured.

"What's the problem?" Eva asked.

"We've been looking for months, and the places we've found have one of two problems—"

"I know," Eva chimed in. "Either the rent is more than we can afford, or the place is in a bad location."

"Exactly. I fear we might not be able to open our own shop." Jena hoped she didn't sound as depressed as she felt.

"Jena," Eva said, "why don't you ask your Sabbath God to help you?"

"Well, OK," Jena said, cheering up a bit. "I'll try."

Jena didn't have enough faith to continue the conversation. She was thinking, *I've been trying so hard, looking for places and working overtime to earn money to start my own business—all so I could worship on the right day. Why isn't the Sabbath God helping me? Am I worshiping the right God?*

She decided she would put the God she was now getting to know to a test. She prayed, "Sabbath God, forgive me. I don't know how to pray to an invisible God. I can't see You." She tried to figure out what to say. Thinking she should be frank, Jena said, "My partner teased me about praying to You. If You're real, please help me find an affordable, good location to start my business so I can keep Your day holy. If You do, I'll believe You're really real, amen."

Two days later, the phone rang. It was a long-distance call from Chicago. Aimee, a former colleague of Jena's, was on the line. She asked Jena, "Are you interested in buying my Jade Beauty Centre in downtown Tsim Sha Tsui?"

Was she? Of course she was! Aimee told Jena that she'd moved to Chicago to see if she could open a successful business there. "My business here is thriving, so I want to sell," the former colleague concluded. When Aimee told Jena the price that she wanted, Jena almost dropped the phone—to her surprise, her former colleague was asking only one-third of the market price. She and Eva could afford that.

Jena thought to herself, *What an awesome God we have. I really, truly believe that the invisible Sabbath God is a living God.*

Jena and Eva bought the business; Jena worked Sundays and Eva worked Saturdays. Because Jena was just a baby believer and didn't yet understand about not being yoked with unbelievers in business ventures that operate on Sabbath, God blessed Jena; and the Jade Beauty Centre grew and became successful.

# The Circling White Dove

In a Philippine village lived a very old man. He was 115 years old—at least that was the age most people in the village thought he was. This old man loved to sit on his front porch and read.

One day a traveling book salesman visited town and went to the home of this old man. He showed him a copy of *The Great Controversy,* written by Ellen G. White. He had no trouble selling a copy to the old book lover.

After the salesman left town, the old man sat on his front porch, opened the book, and began to read. Immediately, he noticed the strangest thing. A white dove flew from the garden to the porch where the old man was sitting. Then, strangely enough, the dove began circling over his head.

The old man thought to himself, *How peculiar. I've lived in this old world one hundred fifteen years—so they say—and as far as I can recall, I've never seen anything like this before.* Never had he seen a dove circle above his head, let alone one that would do so under a porch roof. The old man read the book with greater interest. He noted that as long as he was reading it, the dove circled. When he closed the book, the bird flew away.

The next morning the old man again sat on the porch, opened his new book, and began to read. Almost immediately, the white dove flew in from the garden and began flying around his head again. When he put the book away, the bird flew back to the garden.

The following day, the same thing happened. The old man concluded that the dove liked the book because it came only when he was reading it.

One day, when the old man was in town, he told some of the townsfolk, "The new book I bought is very special."

"How so?" someone asked.

"Every time I open it, a dove flies to the porch and circles over my head!" he replied.

The townsfolk respected the old man very much because a man of 115 years has had many experiences and, as a result, knows many things. But when he told them about the circling dove, some said, "My friend, are you sure you weren't seeing things?"

The old man thought for a moment, then flashed a wise smile and answered, "I may be seeing things. The best way to find out whether what I'm saying is true is to come and see for yourself."

The next day a group of townsfolk came to the old man's house. He met them on his porch with *The Great Controversy* in his hand, sat in his chair, opened the book, and began reading aloud to them.

Suddenly, one of the townsfolk shouted, "Look, up in the sky!"

"What is it?" Everyone looked where he was pointing.

"It's a dove," someone gasped. The white dove flew high overhead. It dove down to the porch and began circling around the old man's head until he finished reading. When he closed the book, the bird flew away.

The next day the old man was too tired to read aloud, so his helpful neighbor volunteered to read the book to the townsfolk. All the while that the book was being read, the dove circled over the old man's head. This happened many days. Then the bird stopped coming.

One day the old man opened to a chapter about the Sabbath and began reading aloud. Suddenly, the bird flew up from the garden and seemed to speak. The old man heard the dove talk. It said clearly, "Keep the Sabbath."

Immediately, the old man knew the bird meant the seventh day because he had just read about it in the chapter. He decided that the bird liked the Sabbath, so it seemed right to keep it.

A miracle like this was shocking to these townsfolk. But their Catholic background helped them believe in miracles. When the bird told them to keep the Sabbath and the book said the same, they looked for a church that kept the seventh day.

It was not easy in the Philippines, because most of the population is Catholic or Muslim, and people attend Mass on Sunday or worship in the mosque on Friday. But the dove and the book said to keep the Sabbath. The old man and his guests decided, "We'll form our own church."

"What shall we call it?" the old man asked.

After some discussion, they named their church the True Church of Jesus Christ. Then one of the townsfolk spoke up, "Didn't the book talk about baptism by immersion?"

The townsfolk looked at each other. "We're Catholic," they murmured. "None of us have been baptized; we've been sprinkled."

The group discussed baptism. "Who should do it?" they asked. Eventually, they decided that the old man would baptize his helpful neighbor, the one who had, from time to time, read to them whenever the old man grew tired, and then the helpful neighbor would baptize the rest.

And that's exactly what they did.

Soon the new church was meeting every Sabbath with the old man and his helpful neighbor alternately presiding over the services.

When the bookseller returned to town months later, he was surprised to discover an eighteen-member church that worshiped on the seventh day of the week, calling itself the True Church of Jesus Christ. The members welcomed him heartily when the old man introduced him as the man who had sold him *The Great Controversy*.

Eagerly, they asked him to teach them more. He told them there was a church in the Philippines that did hold services on Sabbath. The members, he said, called themselves Seventh-day Adventists.

The old man asked, "Do they follow all the teachings in *The Great Controversy*?"

Smiling broadly, the bookseller assured them that they did.

"Could you request a Seventh-day Adventist pastor to move to our town and serve us?" the members asked. "We could learn much from such a man."

The bookseller was more than happy to help. Before long, an Adventist pastor arrived. Today, there is still a congregation of Adventists in the town. They're proud to say that their church began because of a book and a white dove that circled over an old man's head and told him to keep the Sabbath.

They love *The Great Controversy* and say that even though Ellen G. White has been dead since 1915, her message is still very much alive.

# Golden Halo Around the Fourth

**R**inging in the air everywhere could be heard the words "Jesus is coming! Are you ready to meet the Bridegroom?"

One thing was certain in New England. It was almost impossible not to know about the preaching of William Miller. Agree or not, people knew his message. His followers, called Millerites, visited their neighbors, brought out their Bibles, and explained why they believed that Jesus was coming soon and shared the joy that would be theirs when they'd meet Jesus and be taken to heaven to live with Him forever. Consequently, the number of Miller's followers grew.

But not everyone was excited. Many mocked and joked about the millennial excitement. Cartoons in newspapers jeered at the Millerites, asking what they'd do when the appointed day of Jesus' coming turned out to be just another day. If the world didn't end on October 22, what then?

One widow, who'd just moved to the little town of Washington, New Hampshire, found herself in neither camp. While she was skeptical of the movement, she appreciated their careful study of the Bible. Whenever the Millerites visited her home, she listened respectfully to them,

then tried to steer them to the fourth commandment, but without suc-
cess. The widow's name was Rachel Oakes. She thought that Jesus
wouldn't return for the Millerites on the expected day as long as they
continued to worship on Sunday.

Widow Oakes was a Seventh Day Baptist from New York, who'd
moved to New Hampshire to live with her daughter, Rachel Delight
Oakes Farnsworth, who was working in the state as a school teacher. For
about two centuries, the Seventh Day Baptists of North America had felt
it was their duty to keep the Lord's holy Sabbath rather than to share it,
but their attitude changed. In 1843, at the General Conference of Seventh Day Baptists, Rachel Oakes's church leaders were afraid that the
Sunday law might soon be issued, so they encouraged their members to
spread the news that the Lord's holy Sabbath was *not* the pope's Sunday.

It was to share this Sabbath message that the widow had moved to
New Hampshire.

Most of the Millerites gathered for worship in their chapels on Sunday morning. It was no different in the little town of Washington, New
Hampshire. In fact, there were no Sabbath keepers in the widow's new
neighborhood, so she and her daughter worshiped at home. For fellowship, however, Rachel Oakes attended the Sunday services of a Methodist
circuit rider named Frederick Wheeler, who believed and shared Miller's
biblical teachings from his pulpit.

One Sunday in the spring of 1844, Pastor Wheeler was preparing his
congregation for the Communion service. As he explained 1 Corinthians
11:27, he said Paul declared that "all who confess communion with
Christ in such a service as this should be ready to obey God and keep His
commandments in all things."

When Rachel heard those words, she was tempted to stand up in
church, point her finger at Pastor Wheeler, and declare, "Then you're
unworthy to take part in Communion because you don't follow all the
commandments yourself." Being a woman of prudence, however, she
resisted the urge. Instead, she waited for a time when she could speak
with Pastor Wheeler privately.

Not long afterward, as any good circuit rider worth his salt would do,
Pastor Wheeler paid a visit to Rachel Oakes. Before he could get too
comfortable in the Oakeses' home, the widow, as direct in her speech as

she was in her gaze, came straight to the point. "Do you remember, Elder Wheeler, that you said everyone who confesses Christ should obey all the commandments of God?"

Frederick Wheeler allowed as he did. He recalled looking over the congregation as he spoke and noticing the middle-aged woman almost jumping to her feet then settling back into her seat. He'd wondered about her, which was one reason for his visit.

"I came near to getting up in the meeting right then and saying something."

"I thought so," Elder Wheeler said. "What did you have in mind to say?"

"I wanted to tell you that you had better set that Communion table back and put the cloth over it until you begin to keep the commandments of God," Rachel Oakes said.

Frederick Wheeler sat back astonished, grateful that this widow had tactfully waited to speak with him in private. As soon as he recovered from his initial shock, Pastor Wheeler asked, "What do you mean, Sister?"

"You need to follow all of the commandments, including the fourth!"

"I'm a pastor," Wheeler protested. "I attend church every Sunday."

"You're not keeping the fourth commandment," she asserted. "The fourth commandment tells us to keep God's holy Sabbath," Rachel spoke earnestly. "Please promise me you'll look at the fourth commandment again and read it carefully and decide for yourself."

Her statement cut him to the quick. He knew her to be a Seventh Day Baptist and understood her positive views regarding which day was the pope's day and which day was God's holy Sabbath. As she plied him with questions and pressed him for a decision, Pastor Wheeler discovered himself in a tight spot, from which he extracted himself as diplomatically as possible.

Try as he might, however, Wheeler couldn't get the widow's witness out of his mind. He thought and studied seriously. It wasn't long before his studies led him to a decision. Somewhere around March of 1844, he began to observe the seventh-day Sabbath as described in the fourth commandment.

Not far from the church in Washington, New Hampshire, another man named T. M. Preble studied his Bible and concluded he'd been worshiping on the wrong day. In August 1844, the former Free Will Baptist and Millerite enthusiast accepted the Sabbath. New Hampshire now had two Sabbath keeping Advent preachers. However, there wouldn't be a congregation of Advent believers where Mrs. Oakes could attend Sabbath services until the end of the year.

The last chime of midnight struck on October 22, and the glorious expectations of the day came and went. The day became just another number crossed off the calendar. The Millerites around Washington, New Hampshire, had placed so much hope upon that day. They were tired of life on this miserable old planet and had anticipated being caught up with the angels to be reunited with Jesus in heaven.

But Jesus hadn't come for them.

They'd so wanted to see Him.

And now they were mocked by the people who hadn't believed. Many of the Millerites were so embarrassed that they rejected religion entirely. Others went back to the churches they'd attended before—if the churches would have them. Some became fanatically spiritual, while others dug into their Bibles to find answers.

The Harmon family was one of those families who couldn't return to their former Methodist church if they'd wanted to—their church had formally disfellowshiped the entire family because they believed that the soon coming of Jesus would be sometime in 1844. Their twin daughters chose different paths. One decided to set religion aside; the other, Ellen, who, at that time, was a seventeen-year-old pork-eating Sunday keeper, continued her love for Jesus. She longed for the day when her body would be changed from mortal to immortal in the twinkling of an eye, because then she could live with Jesus forever. She attended prayer groups where the members studied the Bible and shared their Christian experiences. Whenever possible, she traveled to share her love of Jesus with others. Sometimes she received dreams or visions that most believed were messages from God.

A young man named James White offered to accompany Ellen in her journeys. Like Ellen, he also wanted to share his love for Jesus and to tell people what the Bible says about Him. Together they, along with a chaperone (often Ellen's twin), traveled by train, by ferry, or by horse and buggy, attending church services on Sunday to encourage the members after the Great Disappointment. Eagerly, they searched the Bible to discover why Jesus hadn't come on October 22, 1844.

About the same time, an old retired sea captain, prohibitionist, abolitionist, and Millerite Adventist named Joseph Bates found a tract by T. M. Preble. As he read it with considerable interest, he learned about the Sabbath. Captain Bates then examined his Bible to determine the accuracy of Preble's tract. Before making his final decision, he traveled from his home to visit Pastor Wheeler. After studying their Bibles together, Bates was convinced.

On the way back home, as he was crossing the bridge between New Bedford and Fair Haven, Massachusetts, he met a fellow Millerite named James Madison Hall, who hailed, "Captain Bates, what's the news?"

Bates shouted back emphatically, "The seventh day is the Sabbath!"

People respected Captain Bates; they tended to believe whatever he said. Instantly, Hall replied, "I'll check it out in my Bible today." Not long afterward, he, too, was worshiping on God's holy Sabbath.

Captain Bates became so excited about Preble's tract that he wrote a tract of his own, *The Seventh Day Sabbath, A Perpetual Sign,* which he published in August of 1846 at considerable financial sacrifice. In the process, his personal retirement fortune was reduced to a silver 1811 York shilling. Undaunted, he continued, trusting God to provide. With the same energy he'd thrown into being a sea captain and into furthering the abolitionist cause, he now channeled toward sharing his discoveries about the Sabbath.

One of those with whom he shared his tract was Ellen Harmon and her friend James White. The captain showed them that the Sabbath is important for the time of the end. The book of Revelation points to a group that keeps the commandments and has the faith of Jesus. It's the seal of the Living God, according to Revelation 7, Bates explained.

The argument didn't appeal to Ellen Harmon and James White. After studying with Bates, Ellen Harmon brushed off the old captain, saying, "Isn't keeping the Sabbath a little too much?" Try as he might, Bates discovered she couldn't be persuaded. Her preconceived ideas were initially too strong. Ellen Harmon remained a devoted Sunday keeper. Her staunch Methodist upbringing with its "free grace and dying love," made

Ellen Harmon think that as long as God was worshiped one day in seven, the details of the fourth commandment were inconsequential. "Don't dwell on the fourth commandment any more than you would on the other nine," she advised Bates.

James White added, "Christians are no longer under the law."

Both of them told Bates he erred in placing so much in the Sabbath. "Sabbath keeping is for the Jews," they concluded.

The next year, James and Ellen were married. They reexamined the question of the Sabbath, continued studying the Bible, and came to the conclusion that Sunday was *not* the Sabbath. In the autumn of 1846, James and Ellen White began worshiping on the Sabbath of the fourth commandment.

About a year after Ellen White was a regular Sabbath keeper, God took her into vision. In it, she viewed the heavenly sanctuary. "The temple of God was open in heaven, and [she] was shown the ark of God covered with the mercy seat. Two angels stood one at either end of the ark, with their wings spread over the mercy seat, and their faces turned toward it."

The angel explaining the vision to her said that the two angels represent "all the heavenly host looking with reverential awe toward the law of God, which had been written by the finger of God."

Ellen White watched as Jesus raised the cover of the ark; she saw the tablets of stone on which the Ten Commandments had been written. She noticed that the fourth commandment was in the very center of the ten precepts. Gazing upon the tablet she noticed, to her amazement, that a soft golden ring circled the fourth one. None of the other commandments were so marked. That golden halo of light made the commandment stand out from the other nine.

When her angel saw Mrs. White's astonishment that the halo surrounded the fourth commandment, he explained, "It is the only one of the ten that defines the living God who created the heavens and the earth and all things that are therein." It's a seal that marks loyalty to a King. Her angel explained that the antichrist thought to change times and laws and had altered the holy day from the seventh to the first, which broke God's law.

If people follow the advice of the prophet Isaiah, by not doing their own business and recreation on Sabbath, and by making the time a delight, the world would have been preserved from idolatry, her guide attested. The promises of Isaiah 58:12–14 apply to all those who seek the restoration of the true Sabbath. The angel went on to show Ellen White that people need to be called back to giving allegiance to the Lord of the Sabbath.*

Before this vision, Ellen and her husband had already decided that Saturday was the Sabbath. When her Sabbath vision ended, if Ellen White had had any lingering doubts about the importance of the Sabbath, they were completely removed.

Joseph Bates, along with James and Ellen White, later became founders of a new denomination that, in 1860, would be called the Seventh-day Adventist Church. It's so named because its members blend the importance of and the relationship between the seventh-day Sabbath and the soon coming of Jesus Christ.

Seventh-day Adventists began missionary and evangelistic outreaches to teach about the Sabbath around the world. Today, there are people who worship God on Sabbath in 206 countries. Amazing, isn't it? When the Seventh Day Baptist General Conference of 1843 called upon their members to spread the truth about the Sabbath and Rachel Oakes complied, it's likely they never dreamed how far reaching the results of that decision would be.

---

* Ellen G. White, *Life Sketches of Ellen G. White* (Mountain View, Calif.: Pacific Press® Publishing Association, 1943), 95, 96.

# Angel at the Railway Station?

T he Shanghai train station was crowded with people waiting to buy tickets. After reading the board above the ticket counters, the man I will call "Mr. Wong" stood in the appropriate queue. The line hardly moved; yet time was of the essence. Every minute he was late for work meant more Chinese *renminbi**\* docked from his already meager salary. When he considered his wages, Mr. Wong knew there were too many days left in the month after his income was spent. If he were willing to work at the garment factory on Sabbath instead of attending church, he'd be able to balance his budget, but his employers docked his wages in exchange for their grudgingly allowing him to have Sabbaths off.

---

\* *Renminbi,* if literally translated from Chinese, is "people's money." At that time, the exchange would be approximately three *renminbi* to the United States dollar; but if exchanged on the basis of wages, three *renminbi* was a day's minimum wage, so take today's minimum wage and multiply it by eight hours to determine the *renminbi's* actual value.

Most workers throughout China were expected to work on Saturdays, and many employers still think that churchgoing is an excuse for laziness. Besides, the factory didn't want to encourage him to worship Jesus. Hence the subtle persecution. Now his family's hunger grew larger than his income. Against his better judgment, he'd borrowed money from a sympathetic colleague, promising to repay it when he got paid. Now he must fulfill his part of the bargain.

Slowly, he inched toward the ticket counter. Taking a wad of paper money from his pocket, he counted it, separated seven *renminbi,* rolled them up, and carefully tucked them into his blue Sun Yat-sen jacket pocket so as not to lose them. He kept the remaining cash in his hand for the ticket, which would cost a few *fen.**

Shortly after buying his ticket, a shrill, crackly voice announced his train's departure and the *masses*† gravitated toward the gate and stood so crushed together that even breathing was a chore. When an attendant opened the gate, everyone, including Mr. Wong, tried to squeeze through at once. Those in back pushed, making the line stumble forward like a crippled millipede. Once through the gate, they dashed to the tracks. Soon Mr. Wong joined others in the hard-seat section of the train.

The train held more passengers than seats, so some passengers sat on their bags or on the littered floor. Unable to find a seat, Mr. Wong leaned against a seat back. Some passengers bumped against him while puffing on cigarettes and shuffling cards. Others jostled about him, taking out bottles of beer and bags of watermelon seeds and peanuts from their luggage. Piles of watermelon rinds and peanut shells began forming on the floor, alongside empty beer bottles and cigarette stubs.

When the train jerked to a start, Mr. Wong lost his footing. By the time he'd regained it, *clickity-clack* beat the train's rhythm to the ruckus of card playing. Amidst the commotion, Mr. Wong casually reached into

---

* One hundred *fen* equals one *renminbi.*

† The masses are essentially a powerless governed class of folk in Chinese-style socialism, as opposed to the people, or the governing class, who under this system are party members, possessing the right to vote and to pass laws for the masses—laws that the people are not necessarily required to obey themselves, but that the masses are obliged to obey.

his jacket pocket to make sure his roll of seven *renminbi* was still there.
To his shock, it was gone!

Quickly, he felt in his pants pockets, but the money was missing. He
double-checked his jacket pocket to no avail. *Where can it be? On the
train? In the waiting room? At the ticket counter? Or worse yet, was it stolen
in the crush at the track or on the train itself? If so, how can I repay my colleague?* Seven *renminbi* was a lot of money to Mr. Wong. He wouldn't
have that amount again until payday at the end of the month. Besides,
he'd promised to pay the debt today. He couldn't afford to miss his appointment or be late for work. If he didn't return his loan, the colleague
might never loan him money again, and if he was late for work, he'd be
docked more pay!

Mr. Wong pressed through the crowded car, searching for the lost
sum. He looked down the aisles and under the seats and tables, all the
while fearing that a thief had palmed the cash.

"Please, Lord," he prayed, "help me find the seven *renminbi* I promised
to return to my colleague. I celebrate the Sabbath every week, even though
my *danwe** docks my salary. I desperately need the money to feed my family and to pay back my colleague. I promised to pay him today. What will
he think of Christians if I tell him the money was lost or stolen?"

At the next stop, Mr. Wong disembarked, dashed into the station,
bought another ticket and boarded the return train. Back at his starting
point, he searched near the track for his roll of *renminbi,* praying he
would find it in time. He searched so intently that he failed to notice
anyone around him. Just as he decided to look inside the waiting room,
he looked up and saw a young girl looking at him. Her soft skin and pure
complexion made her look like a heavenly angel. Only her slightly with-
ered hand suggested otherwise.

She smiled sweetly and said kindly, "What are you looking for, uncle?" Though Mr. Wong was a perfect stranger to her, by calling him
uncle, she'd showed respect for her elders, an honor seldom found since
Communism had forced out the Nationalist government. The sound of
the term *uncle* was music to his ears.

---

* A Chinese Communist work unit, more like a community unit with a
leader who controls your movements and decisions about life and work.

"I've lost some money."

Reaching into her purse, she pulled out a roll of brown paper and offered it to him. "Is this it, uncle?"

He couldn't believe his eyes! The money was rolled exactly the way he'd rolled it. Eagerly, he took it and counted seven bills. "It is indeed my money!"

For a moment, Mr. Wong wondered if this girl might be an angel in disguise. "What's your name?"

"Mei-ling," the girl replied.

"Thank you, Mei-ling." Mr. Wong smiled at her. "You must be an angel sent to answer my prayer." Then he remembered his appointment. "I'd love to talk, Mei-ling, but I've got a train to catch. Could you give me your address? I promise I'll visit you later."

"Sure, uncle." Mei-ling took a sheet of paper and a pen from her purse. Hastily, she scribbled out her address and presented it respectfully with both hands. Mr. Wong quickly took it. The train blew its whistle as he boarded, leaving Mei-ling standing at the station. As the train chugged away, they waved.

Mr. Wong thanked Jesus that his prayer had been answered, enabling him to both meet his colleague and arrive at work on time. Though he suspected Mei-ling was human, he'd always remember her as his "railway angel," sent by God to answer a prayer in a time of need.

# Playing Sambo and the Crocodile

The doorbell rang. Max walked to the entryway and looked through the stained-glass window in the door to see who had come. Recognizing the blond little girl in blue jeans and a flowery pink T-shirt as his neighbor, he threw the door open and said, "Hello, Debby!"

Debby smiled and asked, "Can we play now?"

"Not now." Max frowned, wishing he could have fun, but duty dictated otherwise. Then his face lit up. "Hey, do you want to play Sambo and the Crocodile with me later?"

"I've never heard of that game before. How do you play it?" Debby asked hesitantly.

"You'll see soon enough," Max said, hoping to pique her curiosity. "My dad's the crocodile and you gotta stay away from him!"

"Why can't we play now?" Debby insisted.

"I'm kind of busy right now," Max replied. "I've gotta get some chores done before sundown."

"What's the hurry?"

Flashing a quick smile, he explained, "I've gotta get ready for Sabbath, the day we worship God. Tomorrow we'll go to church. Tonight we'll have family worship. Right now it's my job to dust all the furniture and empty wastebaskets before sundown."

"Oh," Debby pressed her lips together in thought. "If I help you, can we play before your worship?"

"I don't see why not." Max smiled. "As long as the jobs are done, I can."

"Let's get started!" Debby exclaimed.

"All right," Max replied. "Let's play a game to see who can empty the most wastebaskets." Max told Debby which rooms had garbage cans and where to find them; then they divided the rooms up, counted off, and the race began. It was a little tricky in the hall once or twice as they tried to pass each other, but Debby emptied the last basket just as Max came to the door. "I won!" Debby crowed.

"Congratulations!" Max extended his hand, then remembered Debby was a girl and retracted it before she could shake it. "I didn't want your cooties." Max blushed as he rubbed his hand against his pants.

Debby rolled her eyes as she retorted, "I don't have any germs you don't have." After an awkward silence, Debby asked, "So can we play now?"

"Now we need to dust the furniture," Max reminded her. "My mother always hides pennies where she thinks I may forget to dust, so if you find one under a doily or something, it's yours."

"Let's see who gets the most pennies," Debby challenged.

"You're on!" They divided up the rooms again, counted off, and the challenge began.

When they finished, they counted their pennies. "I found two more than you did," Debby boasted. "That was fun! Now can we play?"

"It's time for worship!" Daddy called. "It's about five minutes before sundown, so everybody stop whatever you're doing, and let's welcome the Sabbath!"

Debby glared at Max. "I thought you said we could play after we finished your chores!"

"We will," Max assured her. "We'll play Sambo and the Crocodile right after worship. Come on," he urged. "Join us."

Debby hesitated. "Well, OK. But I don't know about this worship. It'll probably be boring."

"You won't know unless you try," Max coaxed.

"I said OK, didn't I?" Debby retorted.

"Then sit down and join us," Max's dad said, patting his hand on the couch next to his chair.

Mother came in and sat on the couch. Max's daddy opened *Uncle Arthur's Bedtime Stories,* turned to the story of "Sambo and the Crocodile," and began reading. The exciting story told of a boy who was so fast he thought he could swim faster than a crocodile. When his classmates dared him to swim to the other side of a river, he took the challenge, swam for all he was worth, and made it. On the way back, his classmates shouted to him that behind him was a moving log with eyes. Could Sambo swim back to the other side without being caught? Debby bit her nails and sat on the edge of her seat until the story ended. Beaming, she asked eagerly, "Do you have another story like that?"

"Would you like another story by the same author?" Max's daddy asked.

"Please!" Debby begged. Max's daddy pulled out a blue volume he'd tucked in the chair beside his leg, turned to the bookmark, and began reading about Moses in the wilderness. The people found something on the ground that they called manna, or "whatchamacallit," Daddy explained. If the people picked up too much, it spoiled; but on Friday, Moses told them to pick up double the amount because there would be no manna on the ground on the Sabbath day because it was a day of rest. The day before Sabbath was the day to prepare for Sabbath. Those who didn't pick up extra on Friday went hungry on Sabbath. They learned their lesson, and the next week they had food to eat.

"Interesting," Debby said. "I've never heard that story in Sunday School."

"Do you want to hear more stories like this?" Max's daddy asked.

"Do I? Sure!" Debby exclaimed.

"Then come again next Friday," Daddy suggested.

"I'll see if I can." Turning to Max, she pouted, "Max, you promised we'd play Sambo and the crocodile."

Daddy laughed. "And you shall! Right after we kneel and I pray, we'll close by saying the Lord's Prayer together—"

"Then it's time for Sambo!" Max interrupted.

"Shall we kneel?" Daddy asked. Everyone knelt while he prayed, then repeated the Lord's Prayer. Debby missed a number of lines, but managed to come on strong in the end. "It's time for Sambo," Daddy declared. "I'm the crocodile and you two are Sambos!"

"Let me be Sambo first," Max suggested. "You can learn from watching."

"Dare him to swim," Daddy said. "Tease him, taunt him until he swims, actually runs, from one end of the house to the other."

"Just like in the story?" Debby smiled.

"Except without the water." Max laughed.

"Hey, Sambo!" Debby began. "Bet you can't swim to the other side."

"Can too," Max said, playing along.

"When are you gonna do it?" Debby perched her hand on her hip.

"Any time I want to." Max dismissively waved his arm.

"Prove it." Debby pointed her finger at Max's nose.

"I would if it weren't against school rules," Max turned as if to walk away.

"School rule schmule!" Debby hissed. "Do it *now*!" Debby demanded. "You're chicken, Sambo! *Pock! Pock! Pock!*"

On it went until Max felt ready to have Sambo begin to "swim" down the hall to the piano bench, which represented the other side of the river. Then he shouted, "Told you I could make it!"

"Yeehaw!" shouted Debby. "Better hurry back. It's getting dark."

Max started on his way back to the bedroom. Just as he was entering the hall, Daddy, pretending to be the crocodile, charged from the laundry room with his hands clapping in front like jaws. Grabbing Max, he carried him struggling to the couch and began covering him with pillows and stuffed animals. Retreating from the couch, he explained to Debby, "I'm the school principal now." Lowering his voice, he declared, "We must start a search party because there's a chance that the crocodile hasn't eaten Sambo yet." Turning to Debby, he said, "Start calling for Sambo. He'll reply if he thinks you're getting close."

"Ah, right," Debby said. Cupping her hands to her mouth, she began calling, "Sambo! Where are you?" She and Max's daddy walked around in the kitchen and dining room calling for Sambo. As they neared the living room, they heard a faint voice, "Help!"

"I think I hear Sambo," said Daddy. "Let's call again." They did, and the cry for help grew louder. "Where are you?"

"Here!"

"Where's here?"

"In the crocodile's lair—I can't move my legs," Max yelled, pretending to be Sambo. "I was praying for God's help and heard your call!"

"I think we found him," exclaimed Daddy. "Quick. Get a stretcher." He ran to the hallway closet, removed a bed sheet, and brought it back to the living room. After laying it flat on the floor, Daddy said to Debby. "Grab his legs—I'll take his arms." Gently they placed him on the bed sheet. "Lift up the corners on your end. I'll do the same with mine." Max had a hard time groaning as if he were in pain as they tried to carry him on the sheet down the hall to the bedroom where he'd begun. It was all he could do to keep from laughing as they lifted and nearly threw him onto the bed.

Suddenly, Daddy began tickling Max, who laughed uncontrollably, yelling, "Stop!"

Then it was Debby's turn. Soon it was bedtime for the children, so Debby said her goodbyes. "I had a lot of fun today. I'd like to do it again tomorrow."

"We only play this game on Friday," Max explained.

"Why?"

"Because it's something fun that helps to make the Sabbath a special day." Max grinned.

"Then may I play it again?" Debby looked disappointed.

"You may," Max said. "Come again next Friday."

"I will."

The next Friday around sundown, the door chimed again. Seeing Max peek through the stained-glass window, Debby flashed a smile and waved. When he opened the door, she asked, "May I join you for family worship?"

"Sure," Max replied.

Debby played with one of her blond pigtails.

"Come!" Max said.

"All right," Debby nonchalantly tossed her pigtail over her shoulder. "I really liked Sambo and the crocodile."

"You can join us in the living room." Max led her to the couch. "Daddy will announce worship any minute." Moments later, Daddy bounded up the steps two at a time and dashed to his living room chair. "It's time," Max smiled before Daddy could declare worship. Everyone gathered and sat in their seats.

Max's daddy read another selection from *Uncle Arthur's Bedtime Stories* and then one from *The Bible Story*. Suddenly, Debby interrupted, saying, "I think this book is teaching lies!"

Putting down the book, Daddy asked, "What lies are we talking about?"

"Sunday is the day of worship!" Debby declared. "Everyone knows that."

"How do you know that?" Daddy asked politely.

"Jesus changed the day when He died on the cross," Debby retorted.

Patiently, Daddy explained that Jesus kept the Sabbath and never changed the day. "It was the Roman Catholic Church that changed it," he continued. "You'll never find a verse in the Bible saying that Sunday is the day of worship." With that he continued reading the story, and they played another game of Sambo.

This was repeated for many weeks. Debby loved playing Sambo, but argued with Max's daddy about the Bible. Max began to dread the worships because he didn't like the arguments; however, he was happy to have another player who could be caught by the crocodile or play a part in the rescue team.

As the arguments with Debby continued week after week at family worship, Max felt increasingly unhappy on Friday evenings. If it weren't for Sambo, he'd have hidden in his room and locked the door rather than join in.

Max's attitude did not go unnoticed. Daddy asked him one day, "Do you like Debby coming for family worship?"

"It's great to have someone play Sambo with me," Max said pensively. "Debby loves Sambo too."

"I didn't ask about Sambo, Max."

Max hung his head. "I know, Dad. Didn't you once teach me, 'If you can't say something nice . . .'? So I tried to find something nice to say."

"I see," Daddy said. "What is it, Max?"

"Why does she hate *The Bible Story* so much?" Max asked.

"I don't think she does, Max."

"But she argues so strongly," Max protested.

"So it would seem," Daddy agreed. "I think you're just looking at appearances. We need to look at the heart."

Max's curiosity was aroused. "What do *you* see, Daddy?"

"I think Debby loves our worships and is going to her home and teaching her mommy and daddy what she learns from *The Bible Story,* but her parents argue with her," Daddy surmised.

"And she brings the fight to us to find the answer?"

"Exactly, Max," Daddy affirmed. "She's learning something from every argument. And probably her parents are too."

"Ah," said Max as his eyes brightened.

"Now you no longer see through a glass darkly, but understand clearly," Max's daddy said as he tousled his son's hair.

"Thanks for explaining that, Daddy." Max went to play with his building blocks, thinking his daddy was very wise.

Over the next few weeks, Debby continued attending Friday night worships and playing Sambo. But the arguments also continued, and Debby sounded angrier each time. Yet now Max was more interested in listening to his daddy's answers and the kind manner in which he gave them.

One winter day, the doorbell rang. Max opened it to find Debby's mother standing there with black streaks beneath her eyes where her mascara had run. "My husband's rejected me for a younger woman," she announced. "Is your daddy at home?"

"Yes," Max replied. "Come inside."

Debby's mother stepped onto the slate tile in the entryway and stood as if petrified. "I'll just stay here," she mumbled. Her eyes stared vacantly.

Max went into the kitchen and pushed a buzzer that rang in his daddy's basement study. He rang it three times quickly, then one long time. It was a code for "someone wants to see you upstairs." Soon Daddy was climbing the steps and standing in the entryway.

Before he could say anything, Debby's mother declared, "My husband has filed for divorce. He's leaving me for a more intelligent woman. He thinks I'm too stupid." Tears smudged her mascara, making her eyes look like black spiders. "I'm sorry for all the trouble I've caused you," she blurted out.

"What trouble have you caused us?" Daddy asked quietly.

"Debby tells me what she's learned in your family worship, and I've been fighting against it," Debby's mother wiped a tear. "I've said some terrible things about what you believe and I apologize."

"We accept your apology," Daddy said. "Is there anything we can do for you now?"

"I'm afraid to tell you this because you may think my idea's crazy," Debby's mother began.

"We won't consider you crazy," Daddy spoke sincerely. "What's your idea?"

"I think I'm being divorced because God is trying to tell me something. I want to join your family worships and study the Bible with you."

"What makes you think that's crazy?" Daddy exclaimed. "It's the most wonderful idea I've heard in a long time!"

"So you'll let me study with you?" Debby's mother said.

"Certainly," Daddy replied. "You're more than welcome."

And that's exactly what happened. Soon Debby's mother joined a Seventh-day Adventist church and sent her children through the Adventist schools.

And to think, it all started with a game of Sambo and the crocodile!

# Wrong Turn on Friday

**M**om, Chloe wants to know if I can ride bikes with her this evening," Lydia asked as she walked into the kitchen, where her mother was washing dishes. Lydia grabbed a dish towel.

"Yes, after we've finished the dishes." Mother smiled.

Lydia began wiping dishes and stacking them in the cupboard.

"Don't forget that today is Friday," Mother said as she ran some more water. "You'll need to get home before sundown for family worship."

"I know, Mom," Lydia replied. "I'll be home on time."

"You need to be strong," Mother said as she squirted soap on a particularly sticky pan. "Chloe doesn't like to go home when she's supposed to. If you like, you may blame us—but you need to be home on time."

Suddenly, Lydia's little brother, Nathan, burst into the room, followed by Lilipoochen, the family's apricot miniature chihuahua. "I'm bored," Nathan announced as he heaved a sigh. "May I watch today's episode of *Seventh Heaven*?" He waited for a reply but got none. "What's going on?"

Silence.

Not one to be ignored, he asked, "What are you two conspiring?"

"What makes you think there's a conspiracy?" Lydia tossed her hair and looked at her brother.

"You're drying dishes."

"So?" Lydia retorted.

"If I know you, you don't dry dishes unless you want something." A smile spread across Nathan's face. "What's the plan?"

"I'm going biking with Chloe after I finish the dishes."

"Have you vacuumed the house, folded the clothes, and put them in the drawers?" Nathan shot out the words as if they were from a machine gun.

"Yes, I have!" Lydia smugly replied.

Turning to his mother, Nathan excitedly asked, "Mom, if Lydia can bike with Chloe, may I ride bikes with Brandon?" Brandon, who was just a year younger than Nathan, was Chloe's little brother.

"Have you practiced your guitar lesson?" Mother asked. "And done all your chores?"

"I just have to empty the garbage in the kitchen," Nathan answered.

"Good!" Mother beamed. "That won't take long."

"Then may I go? May I? May I, please, pretty please, may I?" Nathan pleaded.

"Are you wearing your watch?" Mother asked. Nathan rolled up his sleeve and showed her his wristwatch. "Good!" she exclaimed. "Pay attention to the time. You need to be home before sundown so we can have family worship."

"What time's sundown, Mother?" Nathan asked.

Mother pulled the sundown calendar off the kitchen bulletin board and examined it. "It's at 7:28 tonight," Mother declared.

"So do you want me home at seven o'clock?" Nathan picked up the kitchen wastebasket. "Is that right, Mother?"

"That's right."

"Do you hear that, Lydia?" Nathan called over his shoulder as he took the garbage to the garage. "You gotta be through biking and home before seven. That's what Mother said."

"I heard that, little bro," Lydia called after him as she placed a wet dish on the rack to drain. "Just 'cause you've got big ears doesn't mean I'm deaf."

"Don't forget, Lydia," Mother reminded her. "You must get Chloe home on time. You know how she is."

"I know, Mother."

Nathan burst into the kitchen, carrying the empty wastebasket. Setting it back in its usual place, he asked, "May I go now, please, Mother?"

"Just ride around the blocks close to home," Mother advised. "We want to be together for family worship."

"All right, Mother," Nathan replied. "Now may I go?"

"Put on a jacket, and be back on time."

"I will, Mother," Nathan promised as he dashed out the garage door. Mother picked up a dish towel and helped Lydia wipe the last few dishes.

When the last dish was in the cupboard, Mother reminded Lydia, "Remember to wear your jacket and sweater. It's getting cooler now."

Lydia, who was headed for the garage door, obediently turned back to get her sweater, slipped it over her shoulders, then reached for her jacket before calling, "I'm going, Mother."

"Be back by seven," Mother called.

"I won't be late," Lydia replied as she shut the door to keep the chihuahua inside. Hopping on her bicycle, she sped down the driveway and up the street to Chloe's home. When she arrived, Nathan and Brandon were just leaving. They waved as she knocked on the door.

It opened and Chloe stood smiling. "Come inside while I get my coat and hat," she said. Lydia stepped inside. "To where shall we trek this evening?" Chloe asked. "To infinity and beyond?"

"Can't go that far today," Lydia laughed. "Not enough time. Why don't we ride to the school and back?" Lydia suggested as she pulled her gloves from her jacket pocket. "Then we can get back before sundown."

"Good idea," Chloe agreed.

Soon the girls were happily pedaling down the winding road toward school. By the time they got there, the sun hung lower in the sky. Lydia knew she should look at her watch, but she didn't.

Meanwhile, back at home, Mother was beginning to worry. Father was sitting in his chair with a copy of *The Man Who Couldn't Be Killed,* waiting to read a chapter to the children for worship, when Nathan returned all out of breath and announced, "Lydia didn't go around the block. She pedaled toward the school."

Without a word, Mother jumped from the couch, dashed outside, hopped on her bike, and sped down the street, leaving Father to begin worship with Nathan.

Minutes before sundown, Mother returned alone. "Where's Lydia?" Father and Nathan chorused in unison.

"I saw her riding to the gate of the school," Mother said. "I thought she'd turn around and head back, but instead she entered the gate and began riding around the campus."

"Did she see you, Mother?" Nathan bounced in his chair.

"I called her, but she didn't respond. Anyway, she won't be here on time for worship."

"We've got to do something about Lydia," Father said thoughtfully. "I thought we'd prepared her to help Chloe get back on time."

Mother sat thoughtfully, then said, "I don't feel like I'm ready for Sabbath today because now I'm hot and sticky—the fresh feeling after a shower is gone." The chihuahua jumped onto the couch and curled up in her lap. Mother stroked behinds the dog's ears. In a thoughtful voice, she said, "We must do something to help Lydia learn to obey. But what?"

"That's the question," Father agreed.

"It seems that we've tried everything," Mother said.

"I wonder if we could learn something from those *Seventh Heaven* stories we've been watching," Father suggested.

"What do you have in mind?" Mother asked.

"You know how in *Seventh Heaven,* whenever the kids come home after doing something bad, they're grounded."

"We haven't tried grounding her," Mother agreed.

"Of course, in that TV series," Father recalled, "the children never complain because they feel like they deserved being grounded."

"I wonder if it would work with her," Mother said.

"Shall we agree on how long we should ground her for this?" Father asked. "A week or two? I think it should be a week."

"Well," Mother thought for a moment. "Right now we don't know the whole story." She stroked the chihuahua before adding, "We'll just have to wait until Lydia gets home and listen to her side of the story. Don't say anything about grounding until we've heard her out because we might not need to, depending on her response."

"All right then, let's continue with worship," Father said, picking up the book. He opened to the bookmarked page and began reading.

About the time the story ended, Lilipoochen leaped from the couch and made a beeline for the door.

Lydia stepped inside, her cheeks rosy from the cold. The dog whimpered greetings as her tail wagged furiously. Reaching down, Lydia picked her up and playfully tousled her hair.

"Why are you late?" Mother asked. "Did you hear me call you, Lydia?"

"Did you call me?" Lydia asked, wrinkling her forehead. "Where were you?"

"Then it seems you didn't hear me," Mother answered.

"Why would I think you'd be calling me?" Lydia shrugged. "I thought you were at home preparing for Sabbath."

"I was," Mother agreed. "But when Nathan told me you rode toward the school, I rode out to find you."

"Really!" Lydia sat on the chair across from the couch.

"I followed you to the school, thinking you'd still make it back as you had promised, but when you turned into the school gate, I knew you wouldn't, so I called." Mother looked straight into Lydia's eyes. "What happened?"

Lydia slumped in her chair. "It was my idea to ride around the campus," she mumbled.

"So it wasn't Chloe's idea?" Mother asked.

"No," Lydia sighed. "I suggested we ride on campus, and Chloe agreed."

"What did we talk about before you left?" Father asked. "Your mother urged you to be a good example for Chloe and help her get home before sundown."

"I thought we could make it," Lydia explained. "I forgot how large the campus is!"

"You knew that both we and Chloe's mother wanted her back before sundown," Mother reminded Lydia. "What do you have to say for yourself?"

"I should call and explain to Chloe's mother that I was the one who made her late," Lydia explained. "She probably thinks it was all her daughter's idea."

"Do you want to call her now?" Mother asked.

"No," Lydia said.

"Why not?" Mother briskly asked.

"Because they go to bed early on Friday night."

"I see," Mother said.

"I think it'd be best for me to call them tomorrow morning and apologize before they go to church," Lydia explained.

"Your father and I were thinking of grounding you—" Mother began.

"The way they do in *Seventh Heaven*," Lydia interrupted.

"Yes," Mother looked at Father, who nodded. "But we like your response. Your attitude is good, Lydia. We'll see what you do in the morning."

"If you remember to call," Father added, "then we won't ground you this time."

The next day on the way to church, Father asked, "Did you call Chloe's mother this morning?"

"Yes, I did," Lydia replied matter-of-factly. "I set my alarm extra early just to do it."

"Good!" Father said. "What did Chloe's mother say?"

"She thought it was very courageous of me to call and admit the blame, and she accepted my apology."

"Good girl," exclaimed Mother. "We're proud of you. You did the right thing!"

"Something tells me you're not going to be late to sundown worship again," Father said reassuringly.

"Oh, I won't, Daddy," Lydia replied.

And, to be quite honest, she never was.

# Adventure at Petra*

**T**ime to wake up so you can eat and explore more of Petra—that rose-red city as old as time!" Roxy's mom called.

"Mom, don't forget it's the so-called rose-red city. The person who first wrote those words had never actually been to Petra." Roxy and her family had just arrived at Petra the afternoon before and had explored *some* of the place, but not *enough* to satisfy them.

Obediently, Roxy got out of bed and started to get dressed. By the time she was dressed and had combed her hair, the family was ready for breakfast. The elevator took them to the ground floor; then they climbed a flight of stairs to the hotel dining room for a continental breakfast.

After breakfast, they walked down to Petra, which wasn't far away.

"Remember," Roxy's daddy said as they strolled downhill, "today is Sabbath, and this is Bible lands that we're going to see."

"The real ones," Mom added. "Not like the theme park in Florida."

"Walking here will help make the Bible come alive." Daddy smiled.

"Didn't Moses and Aaron walk this way?" Roxy's brother, Nigel, asked.

"You got it, little brother," Roxy said. "Somewhere near here as Eli-

---

\* Written by Roxy Maxwell, age ten. Edited by Stanley Maxwell.

jah's raven flies, along with maybe a million of the children of Israel."

"Roxy!" Nigel said indignantly. "Elijah's raven is long dead by now."

"OK, Nigel." Roxy laughed. "Maybe one of Elijah's raven's descendants."

"If we want to take a hike later, we can see the mountain where it's thought Aaron was buried," Daddy suggested.

"We'll see how hot it is," Mommy said. "I don't want the children to get dehydrated—especially since today is Sabbath, and we don't want to have to buy any water if we can avoid it."

"It's a lot of steps for Nigel's little feet," Daddy admitted.

"And it's already hot," Mom added.

"I'm feeling the heat," Daddy adjusted the red and white Jordanian *keffiyeh* he'd wrapped around his head to shield him from the sun. "I'm so glad there's a breeze. Let's do the best we can to get a feel for the times of Moses and Christ through the Nabatean and Roman ruins in the park."

On the walk down, thinking it might make her adventure more interesting, Roxy reviewed what she knew about Petra. It was an ancient Nabatean trading city just south of the Dead Sea in what's now the Middle Eastern country of Jordan. The country's Hashemite king is named Abdullah, which means "Servant of God." To Roxy, the most interesting thing about Petra is that most of the buildings and houses and tombs are carved into sandstone cliffs; some of the carvings are at least fifty feet tall. She had a difficult time imagining how anyone could climb the façades of the sheer cliffs to carve the buildings. Petra was nicknamed the "rose-red city," but as Roxy thought about it, she disagreed, because red is only one of the sandstone colors. When the author who coined that term actually set foot in Petra, he had to admit there wasn't much that was rosy colored about the city. A closer look shows that the mountains are striped almost like a rainbow with just about every color imaginable. However, from a distance, the rocks from which the city is carved do look red.

On Sabbaths the family usually didn't visit parks with entrance fees, but today was different. Luckily, since she and her family were working with Dr. Randy Younker and his team of biblical archaeologists excavating Tel Jalul (a part of the Madaba Plains Project, which is searching for the possible site of the biblical Heshban), they were working for the Hashemite king of Jordan, so they were considered "royal guests" and therefore were granted free admission into archaeological sites anywhere in the nation. The day before, one of the archaeological guides on the team, Mark Zeise, had arranged for them to say "Tel Jalul," and the authorities at the gate would let them in without paying.

So that's exactly what happened when they came to the gate.

After walking down the *Siq* (a narrow gorge that formed when the mountain split centuries ago) that leads to the famous tomb called the Treasury (also known as Al Khazneh), they began to walk in Petra, explore its caves, and take pictures. Turning left, they strolled down the Street of Façades and onto the Nabatean amphitheater carved into the mountain and continued to the Great Temple. Roxy took more pictures than anyone else in her family! One time she had to run to catch up, because she'd stood too long in front of the Tomb of the Obelisks, a beautiful carved scene. She was waiting for a horse and buggy to drive up so she could get a picture of both the carvings *and* the horse and buggy!

*It's little wonder that Petra is one of the seven wonders of the world today,* Roxy thought. On the Street of Façades, all the homes are mysteriously hand carved—and some of those man-made caves make a grown man standing in front of them look like an ant.

As the family walked on, some locals who actually lived *in* caves at Petra approached, urging, "Have your children ride my donkey. It's too far for them to walk all the miles in Petra. It's hot here in Petra, and this is an air-conditioned donkey. Have your children ride my donkey. For you, special price for both of your children—only five *dinar!*"*

With a smile, Roxy's daddy repeatedly answered, "Sorry, but this is our holy day, and we don't buy or sell on this holy day."

"Holy day?" some of them said. "Today's not Sunday. Did you get mixed up?"

Daddy replied, "No, we follow the teaching of both the Bible and the Koran, which says that Saturday is a holy day."

Some looked at Roxy's family strangely until her daddy said, "No, we're not Jews. And we're not Catholics. We're Seventh-day Adventists, who keep the seventh day of the week as a holy day, just as God instructed.

---

* A *dinar* is a unit of Jordanian currency, something like a dollar. It takes about two dollars to make a *dinar.*

He taught us not to buy or sell on the Sabbath."

Most of the time the people would walk away, disappointment written on their faces. But one time, while they were resting in a nice cool cave that Daddy found, a man named Mohammad and his friend Ibrahim stopped and, making small talk, asked, "Do you know the names of my donkeys?"

"Tell us," Daddy replied.

"This one is Michael and that one's Jackson. I call him Jack for short."

Daddy laughed.

"Do you like my donkeys' names?"

"I guess this means you think Michael Jackson is another name for a donkey!"

"No, I like Michael Jackson. He's a real thriller!"

"I'll agree with you about *Thriller*," Daddy said. "I guess you can always sing, 'Beat It' to your donkey whenever he gets stubborn." They laughed. "It's much better than actually whipping him!" her daddy said between laughs.

"Where'd you learn your English?" Daddy asked.

"On the back of my donkeys while talking to tourists," he explained. "I've been giving tourists rides on my donkeys since I was a boy!"

Then Ibrahim offered the same thing the other men with donkeys had offered. "It's hot today. Ride my air-conditioned donkeys, only five *dinar* each. Try and see."

But when Daddy gave the same answer he had given to all the other offers, Ibrahim didn't leave. He stayed to play with Roxy and her brother, Nigel. There was a hole in the back of the cave, and he helped them climb inside and explore. Once inside Roxy was awed by the beautiful color of the sandstone formations in the walls. When they returned, he offered Roxy a *free* ride. At first Roxy thought he was just joking, that he would have her pay later, maybe, after the ride. But, after a while, she gave in and decided to try. So she got on Jack, and Mohammad, who didn't want his friend Ibrahim to seem better than him, let Nigel have a free ride also. He helped Nigel climb onto Michael. And then they started off.

Roxy decided the donkeys were more like heaters than air-conditioners because she found that riding on Jack made her hotter rather than cooler.

Roxy had learned that some people in Jordan have remarkable skill in making pictures by pouring several colors of sand into a bottle. In Amman, she'd watched a man make one for her in the *Suq* (pronounced *sook*), a traditional Arab marketplace, but she felt that she couldn't be sure that the sand in the bottles made in Amman was from Petra. It could have come from anywhere in Jordan. She wanted to go into one of the shops in one of the caves in Petra and watch the locals make pretty pictures as they poured sand into bottles. However, as it was the Sabbath, she waited for sundown. But, by that time, many of the dealers had closed down, and there wasn't time to make the bottles before it was too dark to walk back home to bed.

The next morning, Roxy rose early. Dr. Randy Younker, the dig director at Tel Jalul, had arranged for a bus to take the team back from Petra to Amman to continue work on the tel. "Daddy, do you think we have enough time to make a sand bottle before we go?"

"If you get up promptly, eat fast, and pack quickly, I think we'll have time," Daddy replied. Roxy quickly got ready and ate breakfast in record time, then asked. "Now may we go?" The answer was Yes.

So off they went down the street to find a souvenir shop in the *suq*.

Roxy walked into a shop selling sand bottles and found an artist ready to make one for her. She asked him to put her name on one side and write Petra on the other side. She watched while he put some glue on the bottle in letters that spelled out her name. Then he poured black sand into the bottle to color the glue and tipped any that hadn't adhered to the glue back into his bowl of black sand. Surrounding the black bowl were other bowls with various colors of sand. Then he grabbed a rodlike tool and used it to shape the variously colored sand into different parts of the picture. He used a funnel to pour the variously colored sand into the bottle. As he poured, he used the end of the funnel like a knife to form awesome camels, rugged mountains, and birds in flight.

While the sand was pouring in, the bus drove up and the members of the archaeological dig began boarding. Soon they had made a head count and Roxy and her dad heard them calling, "Maxwell family! It's time to go."

"We're coming!" Daddy called. "As soon as the sand bottle is finished! He's almost done."

Soon it was finished. The artist poured glue into the sand at the top so that it wouldn't fall out. He turned the bottle upside down to show that the picture was secure, cautioned Roxy not to shake it vigorously or she'd ruin the picture, placed it in a plastic bag, and handed it to her with a smile.

Dashing back to the hotel, they grabbed their bags. "Quick. Put your precious sand bottle in your red backpack so it won't get lost," Daddy suggested.

"I'm not ready to pack it yet," Roxy replied. "It's too precious to me," Roxy replied as she put her backpack on. Snatching the bag with the sand bottle inside, she ran to the bus. When she found her seat, she carefully placed the bag with the bottle in the overhead compartment.

"Are you sure you want to put it there?" Daddy asked. "You might forget it. Why don't you pack it in your bag so you have fewer things to remember to take when we leave?"

"Oh, don't worry, Daddy," replied Roxy. "I won't forget it. Trust me!"

"If you're sure," Daddy said.

"I'm sure I'm sure," Roxy answered.

So off they went. It took about half a day by bus to drive from Petra

back to Amman. Over the next week, the archaeologists continued digging at the site. Mommy showed Roxy how to tag the artifacts found on the dig. She painted a little spot on the object, then, with India ink, gave the object a unique letter and number combination, then painted clear fingernail polish over the top so that the ink wouldn't smear. Roxy had found several pieces of broken pottery on the surface of the tel, and her mommy used the same system to identify her treasures.

All too soon it was time for the Maxwells to pack up to return to Michigan. Mommy packed Roxy's sand bottles carefully. She wrapped them in newspaper and stuffed them into shoes.

But when Roxy got back to her home in Berrien Springs, Michigan, she couldn't find the sand bottle that said Petra. She'd gotten three sand bottles in Jordan—one that said Amman, another that said Jordan, and a third, her favorite, that said Petra. But when she returned from Jordan, she found only two of her sand bottles in the luggage. Roxy looked in all the shoes where her mom had lovingly packed all the sand bottles— but one was missing—the one from Petra. That bottle cost thee *dinars*— almost five dollars of her hard-earned cash, gone! Oh, the memories!

Roxy considered that she might never have another chance to get such a bottle again. A tear welled up in her eye.

That night Roxy told Jesus about it and asked Him if He could somehow give her back her sand bottle.

A few days later, when Roxy was playing outside, her mommy opened up the kitchen window and called, "Roxy!"

Roxy didn't hear and continued swinging on her swing set until her mommy called again. "What?" she replied.

"Time to come in."

She strolled slowly into the house. Once she was inside, her mom pulled her aside and said, "Close your eyes."

"Why?" Roxy asked.

Mommy laughed. "Just close your eyes and open your hands. I've got a surprise for you."

When Roxy shut her eyes and reached out her hands, her mommy put something into them, and guess what it was. That's right—it was the missing sand bottle!

# Tested Among the Troops

## Part 1: Fettered in the Guardhouse

For eight years, Pedro had served his father as a *gaucho,* herding sheep during daylight, then selling Christian books door-to-door to fellow German settlers who also farmed in the plains of Argentina. His father entertained high hopes that his son, with his skills, would take over the family farm, but Pedro had other ideas. He wanted an education so he could share what he had learned in his Bible studies. Pedro knew his father wouldn't be happy. Nor would he be easily persuaded, but Pedro had to tell him. That night he prayed, asking God for wisdom and for the right words that could persuade his father to allow him to study at college.

In the morning, he asked his three brothers to help him talk to his father about his goals. They agreed, adding that it wouldn't be easy, but if God wanted him to go, their father would agree.

Together they told him of Pedro's plan, but all his father would talk about was his ranches, all the work that needed to be done on them, and Pedro's work experience as a ranch supervisor. "Why throw all that *gaucho* knowledge away?" he asked.

"But Papa," Pedro explained, weeping as he begged for permission, "God is calling me. I feel it in my bones. I must go and learn how to help others who don't know what we know." After a two-hour discussion, Pedro's father reluctantly consented.

Three months after Pedro had enrolled at an Adventist college in Libertador San Martín, his hopes of becoming a teacher were deferred indefinitely when he was drafted into the Argentine army. Argentina has compulsory military service, but only those names drawn in a lottery have to serve. His notice demanded that he report for duty in six weeks to an artillery regiment in Diamante.

*What terrible timing!* Pedro thought. He'd just started on the course that he felt the Lord had chosen for him; now he was forced to take an unwanted detour. Three months didn't seem very long to be in school. *God's ways seem murky at best,* Pedro concluded.

Two of Pedro's brothers had already been drafted and had served their time. When he talked with them, they had some bad news for him. "You can't keep Sabbath in the army."

"But I must serve God," Pedro insisted. "I must observe the Sabbath commandment even in the army." His brothers and all his Adventist friends shook their heads and reiterated, "Wait 'til you're in the service. You'll see. It's impossible."

Pedro searched his heart. Often, as the deadline for his appointment with the military approached, he walked in the fields alone at night and prayed. Knowing about the strictness of military discipline, he felt that he was facing a life-or-death decision, yet he determined to keep God's Sabbath.

After two weeks of sleepless nights filled with dread, on August 15, he showed up at his appointed station in the river port town of Diamante, located only twelve miles from his school.

His term of service was for two years, but it soon became obvious that he might not return home as expected. It all started when Pedro respectfully requested permission to worship on Saturday, God's Sabbath. On his

very first day of duty, he asked to speak to the commander, stood at atten
tion in front of his desk, and explained why he needed to be exempt from
working on the Sabbath.

"Who put those crazy ideas into your head!" shouted his commander.

As politely as possible, Pedro explained, providing texts from Scripture
to bolster his position. "So you see, sir," he concluded, "this explains why
I cannot work on the Sabbath."

"The Bible's a good Book," conceded the commander. "But you're in
the army now, and it's impossible for you to have Sabbaths free."

"I want to be a good soldier," Pedro answered. "I love my country and
I don't want to disobey, but—"

"But what?" the commander interrupted. "This had better be good,
Private!"

"But," Pedro continued, undeterred. "I can't go against God's command to remember the Sabbath day and keep it holy."

Eyeing Pedro contemptuously, the commanding officer sneered,
"Young man, you're in the army now. That means you'd better leave your
religious scruples behind and obey the orders of your superiors."

"Which is why I'm requesting permission to worship on God's holy
day, sir."

Smiling, his commanding officer replied, "Private, it's your first week,
so I presume you think you're still a civilian, but you're not. You're in the
army now, and you and the rest of the men in your unit all belong to me."

"I understand, sir," said Pedro.

"It's your duty to do as I say," the commander continued.

"I understand, sir," Pedro said.

"We work together."

"Yes, sir," saluted Pedro.

"As a team," the commander added for emphasis.

"Yes, sir," Pedro affirmed.

With a penetrating gaze, the commander looked Pedro in the eye.
"What kind of army would we have if we granted each private his every
whim? I assure you that discipline would break down quickly, and our
forces would be compromised. Permission denied."

Pedro insisted, "It's with all due respect, sir, that I ask my request be
granted."

"Request denied."

"I assure you I'll obey your orders, sir," said Pedro.

"I'm glad to hear it, Private."

"However, sir, if you ask me to break one of God's laws, I'll need to obey God, sir."

"My answer remains the same. You'll show up for duty tomorrow and obey my orders."

"I'll obey your orders from Sunday until sundown Friday, sir, but I cannot obey your orders on Sabbath unless they're to grant me permission to worship God."

After spending time patiently trying to convince Pedro to report for duty on Saturday, the commanding officer grew angry. "Be warned that if you don't obey orders, you'll be punished. Dismissed!"

Turning to Pedro's captain, the commander ordered, "Instruct this raw country bumpkin in military rules and penal code!" Pedro spent the rest of the day listening to long hours of army rules and to the consequences of disobedience. There were further explanations that disobedience leads to disorder in the military, which could not be tolerated under any circumstances. The captain tried to instill a military spirit into Pedro's heart and to convince him that, for the greater good, his conscientious scruples must be put aside.

That Friday, Pedro walked to the commander's office to file a request to have Sabbath off. It was summarily denied.

The next morning, Pedro did not report for duty. His commanding officer found him trying to worship. "What did I tell you about your duty?"

"Your orders were to be obeyed, sir," Pedro answered.

"That's correct, Private. What are you doing here?"

"Doing my best to worship God, sir."

"You're in the army now. You obey me! That's how the army works."

"I understand, sir."

"Then you must go to the river and wash your laundry with the other privates."

When Pedro refused to work on his first Sabbath, the officers formed an angry circle around him and accused him of stubborn disobedience. An officer marched him to the guardhouse, where he was ordered to "Face the wall! Stand motionless!" The commander called an armed guard and shouted, "Make sure this private does nothing!" All through the hours of the Sabbath, the guard watched to see that Pedro didn't contract a single muscle.

After several hours, Pedro was released. When the guard ordered him to return to his bunk, Pedro was so stiff and sore that he could scarcely move. His feet were so swollen that he could barely walk.

Pedro prayed constantly throughout the next week until he felt that God was very near. He believed that God would guide and protect him. When the next Friday arrived, Pedro made a second request to have the Sabbath off to worship. Again his request was denied.

On the second Sabbath, Pedro sat on his bunk reading his Bible. By this time he had become an object of derision among the rest of his unit. Grabbing his Bible, as they often did during the week, they tossed it around the room like a ball, eventually throwing it back at him, aiming at his head.

When Pedro deftly caught it, they sneered, "It's time for the saint to be through with his Mass!" In response, Pedro opened the Bible and commenced reading.

On the third Sabbath, the guard burst into his barracks, shouting, "Because you didn't work last week on your so-called holy day, it's off to the guardhouse for you!"

Obediently, Pedro followed. After locking Pedro's feet in fetters, the guard yelled, "Let's see if this doesn't teach you the results of stubborn laziness!" All day long Pedro couldn't bend his knees. His legs and back ached. Despite his robust strength, he fainted once or twice during the day. Each time the guard revived him and shoved him back into the sitting position.

The following Friday, Pedro again carried over to the commander's office his request to be excused from work on the Sabbath hours. After glancing at the form, the angry commander glared at Pedro and bellowed, "Private, you wait and see what happens tomorrow if you don't work!"

The next morning at six, an officer went to Pedro's regiment and commanded, "Take your laundry to the river and wash!"

Immediately, all the men began gathering their clothes for the task at hand, except Pedro. When the commander saw that Pedro refused to obey his order, he grew furious. Commanding that a washtub be brought in, he placed it where all could see. "March Pedro out here with his laundry," he ordered.

A soldier and an officer marched Pedro out to the tub and dropped the laundry in front of Pedro. Pushing Pedro to his knees, the commander ordered, "Wash!"

## Part 2: Sabbath Is Laundry Day

Still kneeling where his commander had callously thrown him, Pedro looked around him. All eyes were staring at him as the commander stood over him, daring him to disobey. A sergeant stood beside him with a long bar of yellow laundry soap in one hand. An officer on the other side stood at attention holding a whip. Silently, Pedro prayed for courage.

"Wash!" the commander ordered.

Pedro's heart beat so hard it made his chest ache. *Surely,* he thought, *every man in my regiment can hear it pounding.* Reverently, he bowed his head and began to pray.

"Beat him!" the commander shouted.

A loud crack sounded. Immediately, Pedro felt the searing pain of the whip. Again and again, it cut against his back while he prayed.

"Scrub!" screamed the commander as the whip, punctuating the point, sliced into Pedro's back. The commander tried to thrust the soap and clothes into Pedro's hands, which were folded in prayer, but failed. Both soap and clothes fell into the tub.

When the whip broke, the frustrated commander ordered, "Bring another one—one that won't break!" Pedro was given a short reprieve while an officer obtained a stronger one. After two hours, with ribbons of blood drying on Pedro's back, the commander cried, "Incredible! I can't believe that in this modern age a man could be willing to be mutilated rather than give up his religion." Turning to his officers, he commanded, "Take him off to jail!"

The officers obeyed. Pedro spent the rest of the day in a cell, praying for strength as his back throbbed. At eight in the evening, keys rattled outside his cell door. Pedro was released with a threat, "Next Saturday you'll work, or you'll never leave prison!"

During the week that followed, Pedro prayed without ceasing. As he carried out his duties, his thoughts focused on God. Always mindful to perform superior work, he hoped others would notice his spirit of cooperation, but to no avail. His work went unnoticed. No one befriended him. Instead, he was the butt of every joke. At night, his fellow soldiers forced whiskey to his lips or filled his mouth with tobacco. Most of his possessions disappeared. Pedro, formerly a hot-tempered fighter, prayed to be mild mannered and self-controlled. Meekly, he accepted their mistreatment. At night he often sneaked outdoors to find a solitary place to pray, pouring his heart out to God with tears. Returning to his bunk, he felt comforted and strengthened.

When Friday came, his fellow soldiers asked, "Are you going to work tomorrow?"

When he said No, they winked at each other. "Poor saint! He doesn't know what's in store for him tomorrow!" they scoffed.

When he lay on his bunk that night, Pedro couldn't relax. With a trembling heart, he lay awake the entire night, praying for strength.

At six o'clock in the morning, the men lined up and headed down to the river to wash their laundry. Pedro remained on his bunk, reading his Bible, when an officer barged in and shouted, "Why didn't you line up with the rest?"

"I already washed my clothes and my sheets earlier in the week," Pedro replied respectfully and resumed reading.

The officer watched Pedro read for a moment, then said kindly, "Then come on down to the river with the rest. You can sit and read your Bible while the others wash."

A smile beamed from Pedro's face as he jumped off his bunk. With a light heart, he seemed to be walking on air as he followed the officer down to the river and joined the other soldiers. Sadly, his jubilation was short lived.

No sooner had he arrived at the riverbed than an officer shoved a pile of soiled laundry into his hands and ordered, "Scrub or be condemned to perpetual chains!"

Tears clouded Pedro's eyes. "I want to be obedient and become a good soldier. But this I cannot do on God's Sabbath! I will not work on the Sabbath day."

As if on cue, soldiers closed in on him, hitting him. Dropping the clothes, Pedro wiped his eyes as a powerful blow knocked him to the ground. When he was down, the soldiers began kicking him. Looking up, he saw an officer approaching on horseback, carrying a horsewhip.

Struggling to his feet, Pedro dashed for the barracks. The officer chased after him on his horse, flaying the whip toward Pedro whenever he got near. For over a mile, Pedro zigzagged as he ran up the hill, dodging the whip as best he could while trying to keep ahead of the horse.

When Pedro eventually arrived at the doors of his barracks, two officers immediately captured him and locked him in the guardhouse. Once again, Pedro sat on a low bench with his outstretched feet in fetters. From seven in the morning until eight at night, he was guarded. That night, he was thrown into prison.

A doctor came in to examine him. He administered a physical exam and a psychological test as well. Finished, he stepped outside the cell and loudly announced his verdict. "He's the healthiest and the sanest person in your entire outfit."

A military judge from Buenos Aires, the capital of Argentina, arrived the next week to inspect the regiment. The officers escorted the judge into Pedro's cell.

"Why is this man behind bars?" the judge asked.

"He's dangerous for morale."

"How so? His doctor called him the sanest one here."

"We arrested him on charges of insubordination."

"What happened?"

"We asked this young soldier to wash his laundry at the river, along with the rest of the regiment, but he remained behind," the officer began. "An officer had to give him a private invitation to join the rest. Once there, Pedro ran from the officer when told he needed to wash like everyone else. We chased him on a horse, ordering him to return, but he kept running. We swung the horse whip at him to get his attention, but he still disobeyed. Eventually, we caught him and locked him up!"

"Sounds like insubordination to me." The judge sentenced him to seven months of imprisonment.

For a young *gaucho* who was accustomed all his life to chasing the cows in the open fields, it was a harsh punishment indeed. As the days dragged by, Pedro longed for his wild horses. If only he could see just a blade of grass on the range. *Will I ever see the prairie grass and be able to look up at night to count the stars?* he wondered.

Just when he thought he could tolerate his punishment no more, an officer announced the arrival of a visitor. Pedro's spirits soared as he wondered who it could be.

## Part 3: Disobeying Dad

Pedro was surprised to see his dad standing at the door. Tears welled up in their eyes as they threw their arms around each other.

"I haven't been able to sleep for two weeks," his father sobbed. "And your mother is sick with grief. Your brothers and sisters are all sad for you too."

"I'm sorry to cause you all so much trouble," Pedro said. "Surely you understand why I'm in prison for insubordination. It does my heart good to hear that everyone supports me in my position."

"That's what I'm here to talk with you about," his father replied. "I've spoken with the commander."

"Thank you for your help. What did he say, Papa?"

"He's willing to pardon you fully."

"That's good news, Papa!"

"All you have to do is work on Saturdays from now on. Otherwise, you'll be transferred to a penitentiary, where you'll be forced to submit—or die!"

Pedro stared at the floor, unwilling to believe the words coming from his father's mouth. His papa took him by the shoulders and said, "Son, surely the Lord will understand that you're in the army now, and He'll forgive your transgression." Then he added, "You can serve Him faithfully after you have finished your military service. After all, the Bible teaches that we're to submit to those in authority."

Pedro's mouth dropped open. *How can I refuse my father's pleas? It's so much harder than refusing the orders of a rude army officer.* "But, Papa," he spoke tenderly, "it was *you* yourself who taught me to keep the Sabbath. How can you ask me to go back on your own teachings?"

He reminded his papa of the story of the three Hebrew captives who refused to bow down when Nebuchadnezzar played the music. "Would you have taken Shadrach and his companions aside and tried to persuade them to how to a golden statue, just as you're telling me how to break the Sabbath." They wouldn't have listened. They preferred to be thrown into a burning fiery furnace than to worship the image. For honoring Him, the three Hebrews trusted God to reward them in the next life, if not in this one."

He spoke of Daniel who braved the lions' den because he continued to pray even though it was against the law. "He could've stopped praying to God for thirty days and resumed his habit when it was legal again, but he chose to spend a night with the lions instead of severing his communication with God!" Then he mentioned Peter and John spending time in prison because they refused to stop preaching. "Remember what they told their religious authorities, Papa? Peter said, 'It's better to obey God rather than man!' "

But his scriptural evidence was unpersuasive. His dad talked with him for another two hours, trying to persuade him to submit to the army authorities. Pedro kept reminding his father that "we can submit to man's laws as long as they don't cause us to sin." Eventually, with bowed head and tear-filled eyes, realizing that his son wouldn't change his mind, the father left, promising, "I'll pray for you, son."

Pedro sat dazed, unable to process his father's inconsistent message. *Even though the Bible teaches children to honor their parents, I'm to obey them only "in the Lord." How could my papa teach me to keep the Sabbath on one hand, yet explain that his teachings were only to be heeded when it was convenient?*

"Ha! Ha!" a guard jeered, jarring Pedro from his thoughts. Then, almost as if he could read Pedro's mind, the guard taunted, "What kind of son are you that you don't even respect your father's advice?"

Pedro's only consolation was his Bible. After the guard left, he opened it and read for hours, memorizing passages.

The Bible told about when Jesus' mother and brothers came to ask Him to follow the teachings of the authorities even though their laws were against Scripture. Jesus refused to listen, saying that His mother and His brothers were those who did the will of His heavenly Father. *If I lose my father for Christ's sake,* Pedro thought, *I could gain a spiritual one in return.*

Daily, his Bible reading strengthened him.

One day, when he awoke, he reached for his Bible, but it wasn't there. Desperately, he searched his cell, to no avail.

"Looking for something?" asked the guard.

"I've misplaced my Bible," Pedro replied.

"Give up your search!" the guard hissed. "You won't find it! God won't help you this time!"

"How do you know?"

"I tore it up and threw it away!" the guard boasted. Pedro sat stunned. Turning, the guard guffawed as he walked away.

Without his precious Bible, Pedro's days seemed endless. His boredom came to an end when a guard appeared at his cell, "Hey, saint!" he snapped. "Today must be your lucky day. I can't imagine why anyone would want to visit a useless soldier like you, but here's someone to see you. Perhaps he wants you to pray for a miracle like turning prison water into wine!" He laughed sarcastically as he unlocked the cell door.

A moment later a friend stepped into Pedro's cell. He offered him words of encouragement and comfort to him, then, just before leaving, secretly slipped a smuggled Bible into Pedro's hand. "I heard what happened, so I brought you another. Be more careful with this one."

Deciding it unwise to openly read his Bible for fear of losing it again, Pedro carefully hid it in his clothes, taking it out whenever he was certain no one was looking. During the seven months of his imprisonment, he read his Bible from cover to cover twice.

After what seemed like the longest time, Pedro was sent to Buenos Aires for a court-martial. He, along with other prisoners, traveled with an armed guard on the lower deck of a riverboat. The delicious odors from the open galley greatly tempted the prisoners. Tantalized, their mouths watered as they watched the cooks take the food upstairs. The first-class passengers got all the food, while the prisoners received none. Rumbling stomachs encouraged already grumpy prisoners to be grouchy.

"Hey, saint!" some of Pedro's companions sneered. "Why don't you pray that the cooks bring us some of that good food? We deserve a meal, too, you know!"

As the harassment continued, and the prisoners' jeers grew louder, the cooks surprised Pedro by handing him a plateful of first-class food.

"Hey, look at that!" Pedro's companions gasped in wonderment. "God really *did* take care of His saint this time!"

Buenos Aires awaited them at the end of the boat ride. Once Pedro arrived in the capital city, a guard escorted him to his cell and remained posted outside the door. Inside the dimly lit room, Pedro waited for his trial, counting the long days until an entire month had passed.

Eventually, Pedro's case came to trial. Standing before the judge, he heard the prosecuting attorney request five years' imprisonment for insubordination.

"This is the first time in the history of Argentina that a man is being condemned because of his religion," the presiding judge remarked. Turning to Pedro, he asked, "Why don't you perform your duties on Saturday?"

"Sir, I'm obeying the fourth commandment." He explained his determination to keep the day holy as required by his conscience.

The judge reduced the prison sentence to one year. "Young man, you'd better follow regulations there if you ever expect to be free again," he advised.

Pedro was taken to a penal island named Martín García, in the delta of the Paraná River. There he joined the other prisoners who worked in the quarry all day, cutting cobblestones for pavement.

Pedro wasted no time in trying to make an appointment with the commander, and on the second day, he was granted permission. As he walked to his meeting with the commander, he wondered what kind of man he would encounter.

## Part 4: Unexpected Help From the Priest

When Pedro entered the commander's office, he was introduced to the Catholic priest, the elderly prison chaplain, who explained, "The commander has been gracious enough to allow me to sit through the interview in case my counsel is needed."

Pedro requested time off from work to worship God on Sabbath. The commander was incredulous, "Nobody worships on *Sábado*! Don't you know that everyone attends Mass on *Domingo*?"

Patiently, Pedro explained, "I worship on the seventh day because that is the day that God rested on after Creation. God reminded us about that in the fourth commandment when He said that He created the earth in six days and rested on the seventh day. He said that on that day we were to do

no work, nor pursue our own pleasure, but, instead, keep the entire day holy. When Jesus was on earth, He worshiped in the synagogue on the seventh day, and so did the disciples. If we follow the example of Jesus, we should spend the seventh day of the week praying to the Father and studying His Word through His *Santa Biblia*."

Looking incredulous, the commander turned to the priest as if to say, "Isn't he mistaken? Aren't we supposed to worship on Sunday?" Seeing the question in the commander's eyes, the priest replied, "Pedro is right. The Bible does teach that the seventh day is the Sabbath."

"Then why do we worship on Sunday, Father?" the commander asked.

Sitting straight in his chair, the priest spoke authoritatively. "The church, with the powers vested in it, took the liberty to change the day from the seventh day to Sunday to honor Christ's resurrection. Centuries later, the Roman Emperor Constantine decreed the tradition into law. The church has been worshiping on Sunday ever since."

"Why didn't I know this before, Father?"

A broad smile spread across the old priest's face. "Read your catechism again, my son. It's all there."

"I see. What about his request not to work?"

Leaning back in his chair, the priest took a meditative look as he began to answer. "Of course, the church wants people to celebrate the Mass and rest every Sunday. And this man is certainly correct to want to keep Saturday as the commandment says." He stroked his beard, then added, "However, under certain circumstances deemed to be unavoidable or absolutely mandatory, the church grants special dispensation so that some may work on the Lord's Day. I can make all the suitable arrangements with Pedro if you'd like, commander."

Turning to Pedro, his eyes flashing with anger, the commander shouted, "I can have you hanged if you continue to rebel! Don't forget—you're a criminal! You have *no rights*!"

Pedro, knowing the interview was over, thanked the commander for his time and stood up to leave. Dreading the future, but determined to live by his conscience, he thought to himself, *I've withstood beatings in the army, so what more can they do to me here? I just have to pray and trust that the Lord has a way out for me.* Before Pedro politely excused himself, the priest indicated that, with the commander's permission, he wanted to speak with Pedro soon. Pedro nodded in agreement. The commander growled his consent, then smiled, thinking the priest would persuade Pedro to work by giving him absolution, and then the problem would be solved.

Pedro spent much of the night in prayer, begging God to soften the commander's heart.

The next day, one of the inmates yelled, "Someone's here for the saint! Pedro, where are you?" All the inmates were aware of his request for a day off to worship and had observed him in prayer at night. For these hardened criminals, he seemed a holy man.

Rising from his cot, Pedro headed for the door and greeted the messenger, who said, "*El Padre* [the Catholic father] called for you, Pedro."

"Where is he?" Pedro asked.

"In the chapel. Go meet him there."

Immediately, Pedro headed for the chapel and thanked the priest for being willing to counsel him. True to his word, the priest took Pedro aside and urged him to be flexible. "God knows that you're a prisoner without rights. You have to work, Pedro. He'll understand. Please, let me absolve you." Politely, but firmly, Pedro explained his case to the priest. Soon the father realized that Pedro could not be persuaded. Placing his hand on Pedro's shoulder, the priest promised, "My son, I'll speak with the commander for you."

"Thank you, Father," Pedro replied politely, though he was extremely doubtful that a Catholic priest could, in good conscience, make a persuasive argument for the seventh-day Sabbath.

For the rest of the week, Pedro joined the other prisoners in the backbreaking quarry work and, exhausted, slept well every night. Weary though he was, he made it his habit to rise early to read something from the Bible and pray that God would help him to keep the Sabbath. Thursday night he prayed more diligently than on any preceding night. When Friday arrived, he wasted no time in trying to make an appointment to see the commander.

"What do you want to see the commander for?" the guard demanded.

"I want to request permission to worship God as God has requested of us," Pedro explained.

"That won't be necessary," the guard growled. "There's no need for you to see him!"

"Why?" Pedro demanded.

"Because the commander has already decided to grant your request," the guard grunted gruffly. "You may have the day off tomorrow and every Saturday to worship."

"Is this really true?" Pedro exclaimed, hardly daring to believe his ears.

"Believe it!" the guard replied. "You have tomorrow off!"

It seemed as though a tremendous weight fell from Pedro's back. He felt as light as a feather as he searched for the priest. "Thank you, Father, for your help," he said as they shook hands.

So happy was he as he headed back to the barracks that he broke into spontaneous song, singing whatever hymn came to mind. He continued singing most of the next day. Seeing such a radical change in him, the inmates asked him why he was so happy to be in such a miserable place. Pedro told them about the plan of salvation.

"The plan of what?" inmates asked. "What are you talking about, saint? We never heard of this plan."

"The plan of salvation," replied Pedro, patiently.

"And tell us, saint, what is this plan?"

Pedro told them about the story of Adam and Eve and the serpent in Eden. "When Adam listened to his wife and ate the forbidden fruit she offered, the human race fell into sin. All of us have done something wrong in our lives. Some have done worse than others—that's why we have prison terms as punishment for people who break the law. The wages of sin is death. Because all of us have disobeyed God sometime in our lives, all of us should, by rights, be granted capital punishment."

"So is there any hope for us?" the more interested inmates asked.

"Oh, certainly," replied Pedro. "Instead of granting us immediate capital punishment, God places us all on lifetime parole with the possibility of getting the death sentence reversed."

"How did that happen?"

"God promised Adam and Eve that someday they'd have a Descendant who would fight with the serpent and destroy him."

"And did God keep His promise? Did they have a Son who killed the serpent?"

"Yes, God sent His Son. It was Jesus Christ, who died on the cross for you and me so that if we believed in Him, we wouldn't have to die for our sins. It's like the story of the woman caught in adultery."

"Tell us that story."

"The Jewish leaders brought a woman who had been caught in the very act of adultery to the feet of Jesus and asked Him, 'Moses said a woman caught in adultery should be stoned. What do You say?' They thought they had Him, because if He agreed with Moses, the Romans would arrest Him, but if He urged the Jews to follow the Roman law, the crowds might turn against Him and the Jewish rulers could denounce Him as an impostor."

"That was a trick question. I don't know which answer I'd choose. Did He side with the law of Moses or with Roman law?" the inmates asked.

"Neither."

"What did He say?"

"Instead of answering their question, He stooped down and wrote the sins of her accusers in the sand with His finger. One by one, they quietly fled. Soon the woman was alone with Jesus. He asked her, 'Where are your accusers? Has anyone condemned you?' and she said, 'No one, Lord.' Jesus smiled at her as He lifted her to her feet and said, 'Go! Sin no more!' So, if we believe and accept His death, we can change our way of life and stop sinning. Then someday Jesus will return and take us to heaven with Him to live forever."

Some of the inmates who listened lost interest, but one man said, "Tell me more, saint." That was the beginning of serious Bible studies. When the Bible studies were completed, the man, who'd been born a Catholic, but who'd never lived the Christian life, was converted. Instead of following a life of crime, which had landed him in prison, he began, like the woman caught in adultery, to live a new life, following Jesus Christ as his example.

For his part, Pedro was delighted. Now he didn't feel so alone in the prison camp. He now had a friend who genuinely shared his spiritual interests.

One day his friend said, "I really understand the plan of salvation now. All of us were sent to prison because we're being punished for our crimes, but God sent you here to teach me how to live again!"

Pedro rejoiced to hear of his friend's acceptance of Jesus as his Savior and Role Model. With a new baby Christian in the prison, he felt that God indeed had chosen prison life as part of the plan for his life. The days passed more quickly for Pedro.

Four months after his arrival on the penal island, it was announced that the prisoners were to be transferred to Campo de Mayo, a military establishment in Buenos Aires. When his immediate supervisor came to see him off, he advised, "Pedro, you better give up your religious scruples in Campo de Mayo. It will be better for your health!"

The priest came to see Pedro as he prepared to depart, and said, "I'm sorry that you'll be facing difficulties again." After Pedro thanked the priest for his part in helping him on the island, the priest said, "No one will be there to help you." Pedro replied, "Father, God will help me be strong."

As he bid farewell to the priest, it dawned on him that, while his real father had discouraged him from being strong in his faith, he had received encouragement from a spiritual father he had never expected to find—a Catholic priest.

## Part 5: The Commander's Gardener

Pedro and the other prisoners boarded the ship that would take them from their island prison to Buenos Aires, the nation's capital. He had very little time to wonder what his fate would be in his new location because, upon arrival in the city, guards rushed the inmates off the ship and herded

them like cattle to the railway station, where they were shoved into a suburban train. The whistle blew, and the train wobbled and clacked down the track toward Campo de Mayo.

Jostled though they were, there were so many bodies on board that they could lean on each other for support.

At midnight, the prisoners were lined up and questioned. "Why are you in prison?" the guards barked at the prisoners. "State your crime! Speak up!"

Some of the inmates spoke timidly, while others hung their heads in shame. When it was Pedro's turn, he raised his head and declared loudly and clearly, "I'm a Seventh-day Adventist Christian who was denied permission to worship Jesus Christ on His holy day, which is the seventh-day Sabbath. For requesting the Sabbath off to worship God, I was court-martialed, found guilty of insubordination, and sentenced to hard labor."

Astonished, the officer looked at Pedro's honest face, and exclaimed, "You've been treated unjustly. Argentina guarantees freedom of religion. You're certainly entitled to follow your convictions. It's a dirty shame that you've been denied your rights!"

Amazed, some of the prisoners in line declared, "God *is* helping out the saint at last!"

From the first encounter with the officer, Pedro prayed that the commander would favor him. On Friday, Pedro made an appointment to see the commander. After the interview, the commander ordered, "This man is not to be required to work on Saturday. Take him out of the common prison."

Pedro could hardly believe these blessings as he watched the commander stroking his chin, deep in thought. At last, he spoke. "You shouldn't be working with the other prisoners. I wish I had the power to free you, but I don't. However, I'll be in trouble if I don't put you to work." The commander paused. "I think I have the perfect solution."

"What do you have in mind?" Pedro asked.

"Are you good with plants?" the officer inquired.

"I come from a farming family."

"Excellent!" the commander declared. "Then we've found the solution! You shall be my personal gardener."

"Oh, thank you, sir!"

Pedro reported for duty at the commander's house regularly, relieved to know he'd never have to worry about working on the Sabbath again. Caring for plants in the commander's soil was a joy. For the former *gaucho,* being assigned to tend a garden even within the walls of a prison was as close as possible to freedom. Pedro applied his green thumb to every corner of the commander's yard. Soon it surpassed the commander's wildest dreams. Later he made Pedro his personal assistant.

At the end of the year, Pedro was released from prison and honorably discharged from the army. Soon after he finished his military service, the minister of war intervened on behalf of Seventh-day Adventists. He issued an order of the day releasing Adventist recruits from Saturday duties. For many years, that order has been honored in Argentina. Thanks to Pedro's faithful perseverance, all Adventist young men who now serve in the military have become exempt from Sabbath duties!

And to think—Pedro's father said it couldn't be done.

**If you've enjoyed reading** HIM BIG GOD DAY
**you might enjoy these stories, as well.**

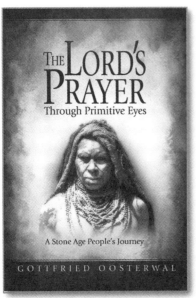

# THE LORD'S PRAYER
## Through Primitive Eyes

From the jungles of Papua New Guinea comes an amazing story of how the Lord's Prayer transforme the lives of a primitive, Stone Age people from warriors to peacemakers. Once they learned about the true God of heaven who sent His Son to die for them, their faith was unshakeable.

Paperback, 160 Pages
ISBN 13: 978-0-8163-2307-4
ISBN 10: 0-8163-2307-0

## Flight 122

The Mosier family's dramatic escape from the flames on April 15, 2008, caught the attention of the entire world. But walking away from this life-threatening plane crash is only part of their incredible story. Through sacrifices, miracles, and answered prayers, God stood beside them all the way!

Paperback, 160 Pages
ISBN 13: 978-0-8163-2365-4
ISBN 10: 0-8163-2365-8

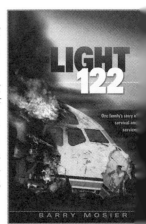

## African Rice Heart

The "dead heart of Africa," that's what the landlocked African country of Chad has been dubbed. But that's not what Emily Wilkens found. Amid the universal poverty, oppressive suffering, smothering filth, and hovering death, she found a beating heart—the heartb of family, of hard work, of fear, of friendship, and of challenge. Emily found the heart of Africa—and realiz it had become her own.

Paperback, 128 Pages
ISBN 13: 978-0-8163-2402-6
ISBN 10: 0-8163-2402-6

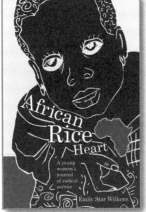

Pacific Press®
Publishing Association

*"Where the Word Is Life"*

**Three ways to order**

| | | |
|---|---|---|
| **1** | Local | Adventist Book Cente |
| **2** | Call | 1-800-765-6955 |
| **3** | Shop | AdventistBookCente |